MasterWorks

MasterWorks

decorative and functional art

MasterWorks

decorative and functional art

Compiled by Sally Milner

MILNER CRAFT

First published in 2000 by **Sally Milner Publishing** Pty Ltd
PO Box 2104 Bowral NSW 2576 AUSTRALIA
© Sally Milner Publishing Pty Ltd 2000

Editing by Sally Milner and Donna Hennessy
Design by Ken Gilroy
Printed in Hong Kong

National Library of Australia Cataloguing-in-Publication data:
Masterworks: decorative & functional art. Woodwork, jewellery, glasswork, basketry.

ISBN 1 86351 276 4 (bk. 2).

1. Basket making. 2. Jewellery making. 3. Glass craft. 4. Handicrafts. 5. Woodwork. I.
Milner, Sally. (Series: Milner craft series).

745.5

Main photography by Andrew Sikorski, Art Atelier
Cover photograph: Colin Heaney glass detail. Photo by Noel Hart

Contents

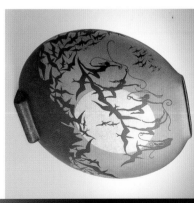

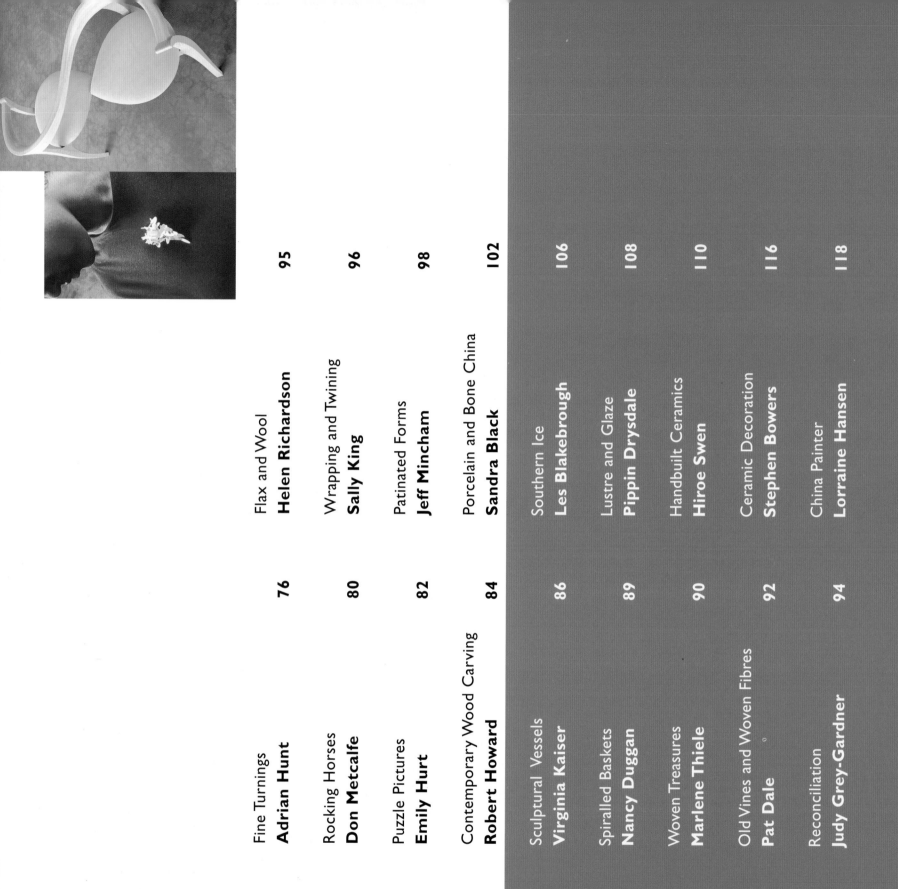

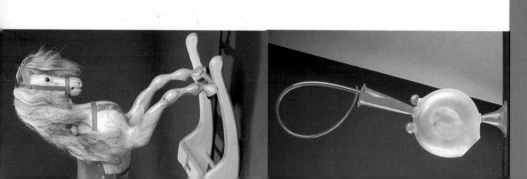

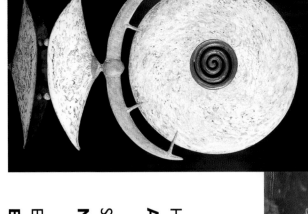

Contents

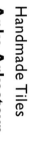
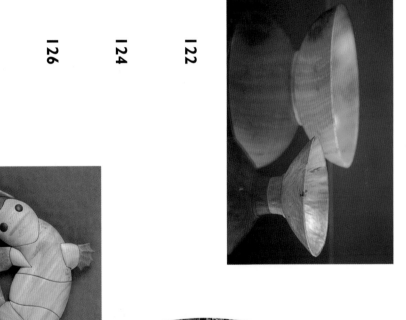

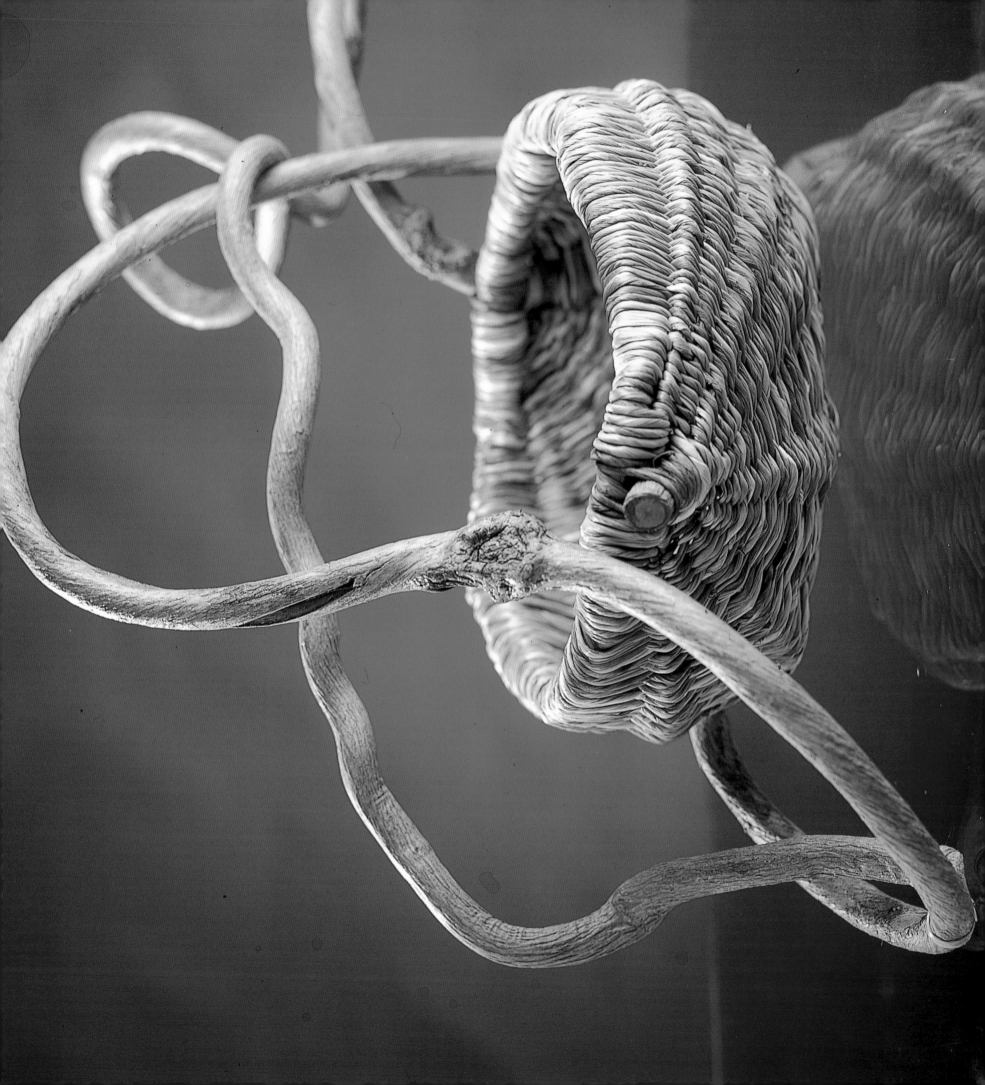

THIS COLLECTION is the result of a request to leading designer-makers to contribute to a book which would display the quality and range of work being undertaken in the fields of decorative and practical arts at the turn of the century and millennium. The response was enthusiastic, and, while some artists were unable to create new work specifically for this project, because of other pressing commitments and our timetable, almost every one was willing to share their work in some way. Some have given detailed instructions on how the work could be recreated, others have given a general description which would enable experienced workers to create something similar, while others have allowed us to display their current work and ideas. All will provide inspiration to admirers, collectors and practitioners. The aim of this book, and its companion volume, is to excite the reader by the extent and scope of the work being created at this time, and we feel this anthology far exceeds our aim.

No collection, however, could ever be comprehensive, or contain a full survey of activity and creative talent today. There are other artists who should have been included. These omissions are a consequence of the gaps in my own knowledge and experience. I apologise to those artists, particularly those new and emerging designers, whose work I may have overlooked.

This volume contains découpage, painted finishes, ceramics, jewellery, woodwork, glass, basketry, crafts with usually 'hard' surfaces and worked by both men and women. The companion volume contains embroidery, cross stitch, lace, patchwork, quilting, textiles.

Ceramics, jewellery, woodwork, glass making, all require spacious workrooms or studios, machinery, kilns and often expensive tools. These artists are committed to their work as a profession, working long hours, producing one-off pieces for exhibition but also accepting commissions and designing and setting up small commercial production runs.

Formal courses of training in these crafts have been introduced into some of the leading institutions around the country, such as the Sydney College of the Arts, University of Sydney and the Canberra Institute of the Arts, Australian National University. Other well-known organisations allow trainees and apprentices to share their studio

Pat Dale Offering basket
37cm high x 62cm long x 29cm wide (14¹/₂" x 24¹/₂" x 11¹/₂")

space and share also the commission and production workload, such as at the JamFactory Craft and Design Centre, Adelaide and the Sturt Workshops, Mittagong. Many of the artists represented here have served in these organisations, dedicated to passing on their own knowledge and experience to others.

There is a high level of professionalism in this group of artists, seeking reasonable rewards for their hours of work and skill, and they have established markets worldwide, either through agents or attending exhibitions themselves, such as SOFA (Sculpture, Objects and Functional Art) exhibition in the United States of America.

Some of the works produced by these men and women are often 'designed in the kiln', or the glory hole or on the lathe, or, at least, during the process, which requires several hours of non-stop backbreaking work and which is often difficult to control completely. Wastage is therefore high as 'failures' are discarded in order to maintain the highest standard.

Skills are honed over years of practice. Thousands of bowls are turned or pots thrown so that some of these artists now make the process seem enviably easy.

Constant experimentation is also involved, as artists work with different woods, different tools, different clays, different temperatures, different glazes. They are always striving for perfection or a new and creative result. New techniques and materials and equipment are incorporated where practicable.

Of course, some artists prefer to 'slow down' their work, to enjoy the labour of hand carving or painting, lacquering or basket making, imbuing each piece of work with their personality. They prefer to work within the structure of a tradition and by constant repetition resolve the details of their designs. Various Guilds and organisations, such as the Fibre Basket Weavers of South Australia, Inc, which has provided training, organised exhibitions and published the definitive book on the subject of fibre basketry, enable members to exchange ideas, to learn skills and to exhibit. Affiliated organisations overseas have introduced members to a wider market and many are recognised worldwide, through these contacts as well as commercial agents and galleries.

The natural environment informs the work of many included in this volume. They are steeped in the colours and forms of the landscape which they represent in their work, through glazes, glass colours, light reflections, or their use of the natural materials, the woods, and fibres, which surround them. Many are fired by the Arcadian dream of a country studio/workshop, and a few have achieved this goal.

Despite inroads made by some of these skilled workers, most live a precarious financial existence. They may take on rigorous teaching and writing programmes, or arts administration positions, all of which keep them away from their studios. But still they continue to practise their chosen art, dedicated to their work and constantly refining their skills and designs to near perfection.

Each one is an inspiration.

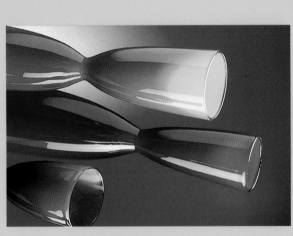

Elizabeth Kelly Hour glass bottles

Découpage on Ceramics

Silvana Natoli

A resident of Sydney, Silvana Natoli studied fashion and worked as a diversional therapist. It was her time in this profession which led her to study and practise different craft techniques. She was inspired with découpage after reading Val Lade's book and acknowledges Val's guidance and knowledge. Silvana's involvement in the Australian and New South Wales découpage guilds allows her to keep up with new trends, projects and developments and, since 1993, she has enjoyed the privilege of teaching others the art of découpage.

Silvana has also had numerous projects published in magazines. She has experimented with many variations of découpage, working on different surfaces, and trying different backgrounds and finishes.

One such variation is Silvana's *Moonlight Dancing*. The girls are dancing out of the cave to celebrate the new millennium. Under the protection of the birds they are heading towards a glorious new beginning.

Crimson lace bowl 40cm (16") diameter

Crimson Lace Bowl

As the name suggests, Silvana was inspired to create this intricate design by the patterns of old lace.

Requirements

ceramic bowl	sea sponge
Liquitex Gloss Medium and Varnish	fine curved scissors
Liquitex Acrylic Artists' paints:	palette for paint
Iridescent Bronze	gesso
Napthol Crimson	wet and dry sandpaper 400, 320, 1200 grit
Cadmium Red Medium	small brush to glue images
mineral turpentine to clean brushes	Blu tac
detergent	water
Meguiar's Deep Crystal Wet-Look Polymer Sealant	10cm (4") square terry towelling
Feast Watson Satin Varnish	varnish brush
lint free cloth	tack cloth
mask (when varnishing and sanding)	Feast Watson Weatherproof Clear High Gloss Lacquer

Preparation

Paint the bowl with four coats of gesso. Allow to dry between coats. Then take 400 grit sandpaper and sand in circular motions, to achieve a smooth surface.

Using a sea sponge, apply two coats of Iridescent Bronze paint to the whole bowl (inside and outside). Leave to dry overnight. This is the base colour.

Using the wet into wet technique, pick up equal amounts of the Napthol Crimson and the Cadmium Red Medium and work this over the rim as well as inside and outside the bowl. Leave the base bronze. Allow to dry for 24 hours.

Paint two coats of Iridescent Bronze around the rim of the bowl on top of the Napthol Crimson and the Cadmium Red Medium.

Découpage

Cut out your images and place Blu tac on the back of each piece. Position these around the inside of the bowl until you are happy with the design.

Take the Blu tac off each image as you glue it onto the bowl, using a small brush and Gloss Medium and Varnish. Start gluing over the rim first then work down to the base. Use a damp sponge to clean away any excess glue from your bowl.

Apply three coats of Gloss Medium and Varnish to the bowl, using a cross hatch pattern. Allow to dry between coats.

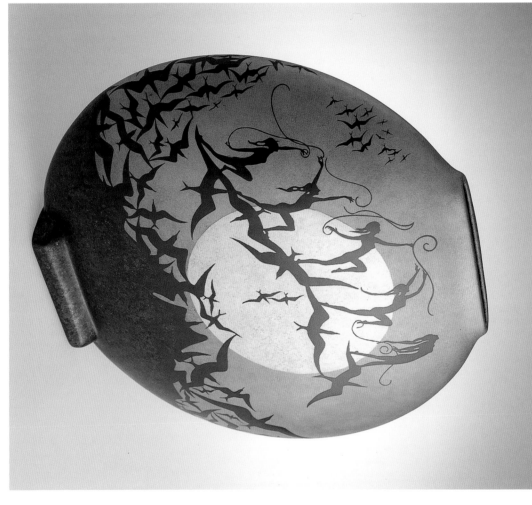

Moonlight dancing
38cm x 38cm (15" x 15")

Varnishing and sanding

Apply a coat of lacquer every day, using a cross hatch pattern. Wipe bowl with the tack cloth to remove any dust particles. After 15 consecutive days, leave to cure for one week. Use 320 grit sandpaper (dry) to do a major sand. This is to cut back the lacquer to the level of the background. Wipe both the bowl and the paper throughout the sanding process. Wipe clean, then continue to lacquer for five more consecutive days and leave to cure. Resand and wipe clean.

Apply four thin coats of the satin varnish to the inside and outside of the bowl. Allow to dry betwen coats. Leave to cure for four weeks.

Final finish

Take 1200 grit sandpaper dipped in water with detergent, and sand lightly over the whole bowl to a dull surface. Wipe clean and let dry.

Polish and buff your piece using Meguiar's Deep Crystal Wet-Look Polymer Sealant and the terry towelling cloth until you are happy with the finish.

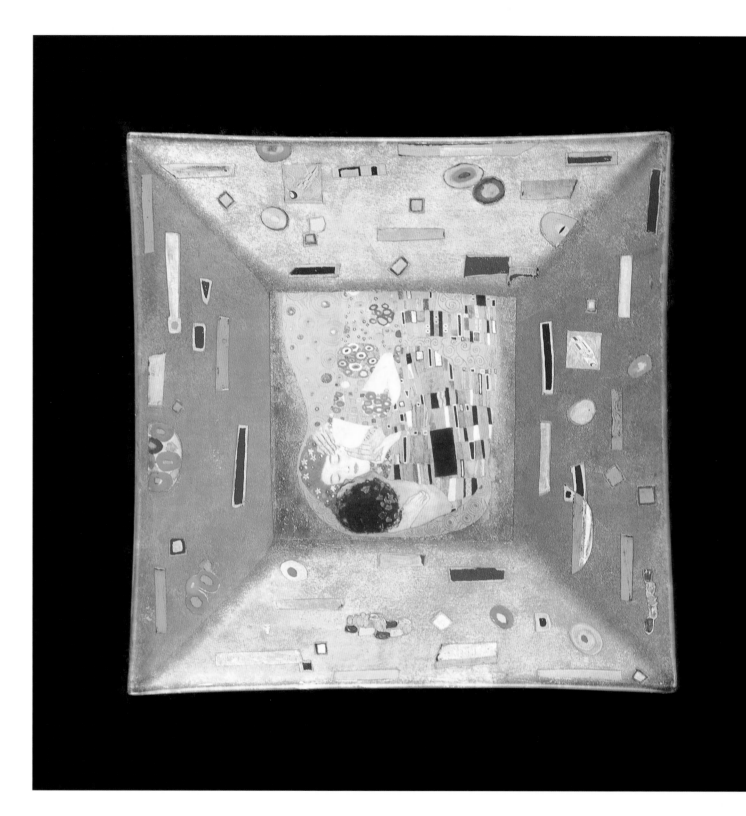

Nerida Singleton

Constantly experimenting with new products, constantly creating ways of improving traditional découpage techniques, Nerida Singleton has been an inspiration to other découpage artists and students for 15 years.

Always generous with her time and expertise, Nerida is willing to share her 'discoveries'. She has encouraged countless others to seriously pursue this art form, including the other découpage artists featured in this book. She travels extensively both within Australia and overseas to teach, her work has been featured in magazines and television and is often seen at exhibitions and craft shows. Somehow Nerida still finds time to create her own heirlooms of the future.

Not tied to one type of object, Nerida's découpage has transformed wooden boxes, chests, chairs, screens and furniture as well as ceramics, glass and metal.

Here Nerida has worked on a beautiful piece of handmade glass. It can be used as a plaque, platter or plate. She has used a print of the well-known painting *The Kiss* by Gustav Klimt who worked in Vienna more than a century ago. He had a distinctive style and his work was often supported by backgrounds of gold leaf. Nerida has continued this theme in her work.

Découpage on glass is taxing and can cause grief if the gluing is not done dexterously, however, there are advantages, the main one being that there is no need for the successive applications of varnish with constant sanding between, which characterises other forms of découpage. Instead, all work is done on the under side of the glass.

Découpage on glass plate 38cm x 38cm (15" x 15")

Nerida Singleton

Découpage on Glass Plate

Requirements

glass plate	*The Kiss* by Gustav Klimt print
vinegar	tissues
Liquitex Gloss Medium & Varnish	foam, mop, and 2.5cm (1") soft brushes
baking paper	fine scissors
kitchen sponge cotton buds	bowl of water and towel scourer
Blu tac	heavy duty water-based varnish (J.W. Right Step)
Siapol and polishing cloth	PVA glue (optional)
Liquitex Artist's Acrylic paints:	silicon carbide sanding pads (coarse, medium, fine)
Iridescent Copper	white cotton gloves
Antique Copper	gold leaf
Iridescent Gold	acrylic gold size (Langridge)
unbleached sea sponge, fine texture	0000 steel wool

Clean the glass with vinegar on tissues. Dry with a lint free cloth. Select the main image from the Klimt collection and have it photocopied to fit the interior base of your glass. The glass frame is decorated with segments from the costumes in *The Kiss* and these need to be increased in size. Nerida copied the image four times to ensure there was sufficient material.

The print needs to be strengthened so it will tolerate manipulation as it is glued to the back of the plate. If the paper is fragile it will stretch, wrinkle and possibly tear. Apply an even coat of Liquitex Gloss Medium & Varnish to the front and back of your print. If you prefer, a second, sparing coat of this sealer can be added to the top for further strengthening. Layer your prints with the baking paper to prevent them sticking to each other.

Design

Cut your print to fit the base of the plate and decide on the composition of elements from your extra copies for the frame. Using Blu tac, place the cut outs randomly around the edges until you are satisfied with the balance of shape and colour.

Gluing

Be sure the surface of the back of the glass has no finger prints or smudges. Rub lightly with vinegar and dry with a lint free cloth. Put a generous amount of sealer on the base of the glass, rub it about until it is silky and has even coverage. Place your print face down on the sealer and, with a small amount of sealer on your fingertips, lightly massage the back of the print to secure the image to the glass. It takes some time for the bonding, and, so your fingers don't stick to the surface of your print, constantly add a little more sealer. Do not stop adding sealer until there is no movement in your image. You will have five or ten minutes, so don't be anxious and hurry. Nerida does the initial massaging with the plate face down on the table, then turns it over and checks whether the image is adhering to the glass. There will be cloudy sealer evident, and areas of light (air bubbles or spots where the print is lifted away from the glass). Working from the middle with the plate facing you, and with your fingertips moistened, trace out the excess sealer and the air bubbles. This will take some time and might have to be repeated.

As you move the sealer away from the centre to the edges, mop up the excess straight away with a dry kitchen sponge. Be sure you do not disturb the edges of the print and ensure the sponge is quite free of water which could penetrate behind the image. (If you do not constantly remove the excess sealer it sets hard very quickly. You can damage the edge of the print if you have to use a scourer or scalpel to free it. Also, the sealer will leave a halo of light around your images if it is not entirely removed.)

Clean away any sealer residue with a light scouring with vinegar before you attach the individual extra cut outs, again using the sealer, but securing only one image at a time. It is too difficult to try to speed up the gluing and the smaller images need time to adhere. If they are recalcitrant, you might need the added strength of a PVA glue instead of the sealer. This will be cloudy, however, and will take some time to dry clear.

Background painting

All the images must be dry and clear before you apply any paint. Again, be sure your glass surface is perfectly clean. Lightly pat a dusting of Iridescent Copper or Antique Copper paint on the reverse of the glass, over the images. The back of the glass is going to be gold leafed and the paint will slightly colour the leaf and make it less 'glitzy'. Allow the paint to cure overnight.

Gold leaf

Paint the adhesive gold size over the back of the glass using a soft brush. If you apply pressure on your brush you will dislodge the paint. The size will be cloudy at first but will dry in about 15 minutes.

Wearing white cotton gloves, float the sheet of gold leaf onto the size and pat to the surface with a soft mop brush to secure the leaf. You may apply the leaf in a closed or open pattern. Hold the leaf at the edges and lightly push the leaf to the surface to remove the square edged look, or, if you prefer a broken pattern, tear the leaf and place it randomly on the surface.

Paint a thin covering of sealer over the leaf to protect it. Then paint on several coats of Iridescent Copper, Antique Copper and Iridescent Gold. This will give interest to the back of the plate. These might need several applications as the iridescent paints are usually transparent and, when you hold the plate to the light, you don't want to be able to see the light through it.

Varnishing and finishing

The more coats of varnish you apply to the reverse of your plate, the more protection you give to your composition. However, six coats should be sufficient. Use a water based varnish and apply several coats, then alternate a light sand between coats to remove dust, brush strokes or air bubbles. Use the fine steel wool around the edge of the glass to remove excess paint. When the surface is smooth and even, sand with the finest sanding pad, which will give a subtle sheen to the surface.

Apply Siapol with a foam applicator. Follow product instructions. Allow several minutes, then polish with a polishing cloth.

(Alternative: The outline of the separate small cut outs will be evident from the back of the plate. It is possible to fill the back with a tinted gesso if you prefer a smooth surface on the back. Sand between applications with a coarse silicon carbide sanding pad and, when smooth, apply the paint combination and varnish as previously directed.)

[Glass prepared in this manner is decorative and should not be immersed in water or a dishwasher. Your dish may be used as a platter for fruit or dry food and a light wipe with a kitchen sponge is all that is necessary to keep it clean.]

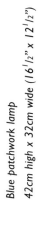

Blue patchwork lamp
42cm high x 32cm wide (16¹/₂" x 12¹/₂")

Russian urn (top left)
38cm high x 20cm wide (15" x 8")

'Versace' pedestal urn (left)
60cm high x 30cm wide (24" x 12")

Beverley Evans

Beverley Evans joined fellow-Queenslander Nerida Singleton's découpage classes in 1992. She immediately became enthralled with the concept of design and composition and loved the challenges of mastering paints, varnishes and glues. Beverley had no training in painting, drawing or other craftwork and was amazed she could master the disciplines necessary for this work.

At first she followed the traditional styles of découpage, then, as a present for a son living in London she created a briefcase with a myriad of Aboriginal art forms. Realising that she was not restricted, she went on to create trunks and boxes with themes of astronomy, Egypt, Russia, sport and geometric designs.

These days Beverley also creates découpage on ceramics, glass, eggs and even soaps. A recent trip to Europe netted a huge store of books, catalogues and brochures, all of which provide continued inspiration.

Beverley does not believe in counting the layers of varnish she adds to achieve her perfect finishes. Instead, she continues to coat and sand until the project is 'flat' and the images cannot be felt with the fingertips while the eyes are closed. 'Then, and only then have you finished varnishing.'

Beverley uses many different products for sanding. If she uses an oil-based varnish she uses 'wet and dry' sandpaper (wet), starting with 320 grade and working down to finer grades. If water-based varnish is used, then Siacar, by Siafast, blue velour backed paper, which starts with grade 320 and moves down to the finer grades is used. For finishing she uses foam backed sanding pads and/or the Micro-mesh system. Like other découpage artists she is always striving for an easier and quicker way.

Beverley Evans

Rose Floor Vase

This vase was quite a challenge because of its size. A great deal of hand painting was required for the background. The wrapping paper used was called *Roses* and was a copy of a painting from around 1820.

Requirements

bisque ware vase	wallpaper paste
Gloss Medium and Varnish	Siafast blue velour backed paper
Micro-mesh kit	water-based varnish
Liquitex Artist's Acrylic paints:	
Maroon	
Green Oxide	
Titanium White	
Burnt Umber	
Iridescent Copper	

The base and lower section of the Vase was painted in straight Liquitex Maroon. Moving up the vase, Green Oxide, Titanium White and Burnt Umber were added. These were not mixed together on the palette. The finish resembles the background of the wrapping paper. Handles and rim were painted in Iridescent Copper and Maroon blended.

Images were glued to the vase with wallpaper paste which is more suitable for large images on bisque ware. These were then sealed with Gloss Medium and Varnish.

Water based varnish was used for this project to minimise colour change as the varnish is built up. Some 40 coats were needed to achieve 'Beverley's finish'. Then the vase was polished to a final gloss using Micro-mesh.

Rose floor vase
40cm high x 36cm wide (15³/4" x 14")

Romantic Découpage

Margôt Hamilton

After reading an English magazine article about découpage in 1992, Margôt Hamilton couldn't wait to try the craft for herself. So it was with great anticipation that she attended her first evening class, to find a group of silent ladies seated around a table, cutting out delicate images with tiny scissors. Her initial reaction was 'This is not for me; I won't be able to sit still long enough!'

Well, eight years later, having decorated objects of all shapes, sizes and ages, collected hundreds of decorative papers, art prints and books, Margôt is more in love with this age-old craft than ever. Découpage has taken over her life.

Four years ago she left the business world to devote more time to her passion. Although not formally trained in art, through the medium of découpage Margôt has found her intuitive talents and extended her love of art, colour and design.

Fascinated by the history of découpage, Margôt has travelled extensively in search of original découpage pieces. Special inspiration has come from visits to Venice. Italian art has been an important influence, particularly the Renaissance painters, as has Italian architecture and the colours of Italy. Margôt has even taken her interest in all things Italian to the extent of immersing herself in the language and culture of the country.

Sometimes a particular piece of paper will inspire Margôt to create a special project around it. This was the case with the *Summer flowers wall mirror*, when the soft tones of the paper brought to mind an Impressionist summer garden.

Summer flowers wall mirror 50cm (20") diameter

Renaissance Table

Margot decided to use Bronzino's 'Lucrezia' on the top of this table. She looked so mysterious and the rich red of her dress was wonderful. She then searched for flowers of the same tonings to surround her and arranged them to suit the table's octagonal shape. The script paper on the sides suited the period of the image very well.

The table shown here had been made especially to be decorated but an old one would work just as well, providing any old paint or varnish was removed first.

Requirements

suitable table   gilding cream

black gesso   suitable images

sandpaper of various grades – coarse to fine fine curved scissors

sea sponge   brushes

Liquitex Acrylic Artist's paints:

       Mars Black   Micro-mesh

       Raw Umber   Satin Varnish

Polymer Medium   Wattyl Estapol Gloss Varnish

The table was prepared with two to three coats of gesso all over it, including the inside. When dry, any rough edges were sanded smooth with the coarse sandpaper, paying particular attention to the edges.

A sea sponge was used to paint the table with a brush for difficult corners. A mixture of Mars Black and Raw Umber was used, and gilding cream was added to define the edges.

The images were carefully glued in place with Liquitex Polymer Medium and two to three coats of this were applied as a sealer over the entire surface and allowed to dry well.

Twenty coats of lacquer were then applied on the top and sides of the table – Wattyl Estapol Gloss. It was finished with a light sand and a final two coats.

Finally, the polish was achieved with Micro-mesh.

Satin Varnish, two to three coats, was painted onto the pedestal and legs.

Renaissance table 60cm
(24") high

Folk Art

Deborah Kneen

A well-known teacher and writer, Deborah Kneen has been painting since she was a small child. More recently, she has travelled extensively to further her studies of folk art and, in particular, has researched traditional forms in Europe — Bauernmalerei and French painted decoration, among others.

Deborah's books are sold internationally to great acclaim and she is an accredited teacher of the Folk and Decorative Artists' Association of Australia Inc. She enjoys painting most styles and subject matter, from portraits to flowers to mediaeval motifs.

Recently, Deborah taught in France — and in the French language, another passion — but her happiest moment in folk art was being made an honorary life member of the Friends through Folk Art Guild, Inc.

Deborah always enjoys creating 'one off' pieces and is often inspired by her lovingly restored old world garden.

In her distinctive piece 'Federation House and Lace Tray', Deborah combines a traditional central motif with exquisite fine lace work to create a delightful platter with that ever-present 'old world' charm.

Federation house and lace tray 30cm (12") diameter

Deborah Kneen

This detailed section of the
pattern is for reference only.
Transfer the basic outline of
lace only, as explained.

Pattern actual size

Federation house and lace tray

Requirements

round box or tray

Jo Sonja's Artists' Colours:

Forest Green (background)	Warm White
Naples Yellow Hue	Gold Oxide
Ultramarine	Aqua (optional)
Raw Sienna	Carbon Black
Teal Green	Unbleached Titanium
Turners Yellow	Brown Madder
Dioxazine Purple	Titanium White
Olive Green	Brown Earth

brushes:

sponge/foam brush or basecoating brush
No 2 or 3 pointed round brush
liner or fine round brush
No 8 or 10 flat brush (a No 6 will do if necessary)

mediums:

Jo Sonja's Flow Medium
Jo Sonja's Clear Glazing Medium

tracing paper

pencil

Scotch Magic Tape

white and grey transfer paper

stylus

ruler

Basecoating and transferring the pattern

Using a sponge brush or basecoating brush, basecoat in Forest Green. Trace the pattern onto tracing paper, bearing in mind you do not need to trace the intricate lace details. These can be painted freehand later using the pattern as a guide. When the basecoat is dry, centre the pattern carefully on your surface and secure with Scotch Magic Tape. Slip a sheet of white transfer paper underneath and use a stylus to transfer the lace scallop outline and basic lace design but not the intricate lace details.

Central scene

There is no single 'correct' way to paint the background for the landscape. Alternative methods are given below.

Paint the centre, i.e. the area where the landscape is to be painted, with Naples Yellow Hue. Several coats might be necessary. Allow each to dry well. Tidy up the edges as necessary with a damp cotton bud. Don't allow the Naples Yellow Hue to go onto the lace area. Alternatively, transfer the house outline and horizon line and then paint the house and sky or house only in Naples Yellow Hue and leave the foreground/garden dark green. In this case, you would use white transfer paper for the garden details.

Realign the pattern and transfer the scene lightly, using grey/white transfer paper as appropriate and a ruler for straight lines.

Sky

With a large flat brush apply a slightly diluted mix of Ultramarine and Warm White, to make a medium blue. Starting at the top, paint the sky with long, smooth horizontal strokes. Add extra Warm White as you move down towards the horizon where the sky is lightest. Leave the Naples Yellow Hue showing at the horizon. Allow to dry. Repeat until the sky looks smooth, but ensure each wash is dry before continuing, otherwise the underlying colour will lift.

The sky colour is a matter of taste. To grey the sky colour a little (particularly towards the top of the sky where it is darkest), add a touch of complementary colour, Gold Oxide, to the mix. Alternatively, to brighten the sky, add a touch of Aqua to the mix.

Tidy up the edges of the sky if necessary with a damp cotton bud and allow to dry.

Clouds

With the flat brush, still dirty with the sky colour, sideload with Warm White, blend on your palette and paint the clouds. Soften the edges with your fingertips if necessary. Allow to dry. Repeat if desired. You can even pat in a little of the greyed sky colour under the clouds –but very subtly.

Path

With the flat brush, paint a horizontal wash of Raw Sienna or Gold Oxide. Repeat. Let dry. With a sideloaded flat brush, float Brown Earth along the edges of the path. Highlight the path here and there with a round brush and watery Raw Sienna, plus a touch of Warm White.

House

Base the walls and roof with slightly watery Raw Sienna or Gold Oxide. You will need at least two coats for opaque coverage. Leave the windows and other gaps in the original Naples Yellow Hue to show as separation between parts of the house.

Sponged foliage and garden

Take a small piece of sponge, dampen it and squeeze out excess. When loading, always wipe off excess paint on a cloth or paper towel. Load with Teal or Olive Green and sponge on the contours of the foliage, leaving the base colour as highlights if you have used a Naples Yellow Hue background. If you have left the background colour of the garden in dark green, adjust the green stippling colours accordingly, working from the dark up to the light. Try to keep off the path, except at the edges, and sponge up onto the base of the cottage as shown. Deepen shadow areas here and there by sponging Olive Green plus a touch of Carbon Black. Build up the sponging in progressively lighter layers (add a little Turners Yellow) to the sponge. Remember to wipe the sponge well as you add colour, but don't wash it out. You need a dirty sponge containing some of the previous colour. Finally add a touch of Warm White to the dirty sponge and lightly sponge the tops of trees and bushes. Hint: If you have stippled onto the lace area or over the house, touch these up with the base colour or remove with a damp cotton bud.

Flowers

Now have fun placing the flowers. They are bigger towards the foreground and diminish in size towards the back. They tend to grow in loose drifts of colour. Note many are just dots. Add stems as necessary. Remember to place a few flowers overlapping the path. You can brush-mix or doubleload colours for extra effect. Here are some suggestions:

Hollyhocks: Brown Madder plus Unbleached Titanium   Yellow Daisies: Turners Yellow plus Warm White

Purple Salvia: Dioxazine Purple plus Unbleached Titanium   White dot flowers: Warm White

Add other flowers as desired.

Floated shadows

The scene must be dry. Pre-wet around the edge of the scene with a clean damp brush. Dampen the large flat brush and sideload with Brown Earth, blend on your palette and float a shadow around the edge of the scene. Don't worry if it goes onto the lace area. Leave to dry.

Shading and detailing the house

When dry, use a flat brush to float shadows of Gold Oxide or Brown Earth. Add linework in Brown Earth with your liner brush – windows, half-timbering, roof thatch. Add shading to the windows with Brown Earth plus Carbon Black.

Lace frame

Linework for lace: Don't worry if panels vary a little. You will notice that Deborah had to 'fudge' the pattern on some of the sections on the circle. They are not exactly the same – some parts are stretched, others contracted.

Mix Warm White with Flow Medium to give an inky consistency. You can add a little water too, if you like – not too runny but not too thick. Using a liner brush, paint all the main outlines first. These will need several coats to give opaque coverage. The finer lines will need only one coat. You may want to go over the main lines with Titanium White to accentuate them. Always roll your brush on a tissue to remove excess paint mix – otherwise you will have very thick lines. When dry, erase lace pattern lines.

Washes on lace motifs: Some of the larger scrolls and flower petals are coloured in with a soft wash of Warm White. Paint these washes using a No 2 or 3 round brush. Add Flow Medium to the paint and wipe off excess mix before painting the wash. You need only the slightest hint of paint on your brush. When dry, paint a second coat if the first is too light – but don't make these areas too opaque.

Finishing

Ensure everything is dry. Erase all pattern lines. Touch up any smudges on the background with the original dark green base colour. Sign your masterpiece. Now varnish if appropriate

Angel with lute
42cm x 29.7cm
(16¹/₂" x 11³/₄")

Julie Whitehouse

The icon paintings of Queensland artist Julie Whitehouse are thoroughly researched and then adapted to modern ideals and painting techniques while retaining the spirituality and style of traditional icons. Indeed, originality, attention to detail, experimentation with colour harmonies and careful consideration of composition in order to produce a visually pleasing piece of art, are all Julie's goals. So admired is Julie's art that she was commissioned to work on Papal Vestments for Pope John Paul II's Australian visit.

A busy working artist, Julie has also been involved in design of greeting cards, theatrical sets, commercial logos, posters, corporate presentations, commissioned paintings, book illustrations and découpage papers. Amongst all this, she also finds time to teach art at secondary school level as well as after hours adult workshops and primary school children's art workshops.

Julie draws her inspiration for designs from many sources. Indeed, her *Tuscan Platter* project was inspired by the ornately painted ceramic ware of Sienna in Northern Italy, where the patterns are intricate and the colours are often vibrant.

Julie has developed more than 100 original designs suitable for step by step teaching to beginners as well as advanced students.

Tuscan platter 50.7cm (20") diameter

Julie Whitehouse

Vladimir Madonna

Based on mother and child icons of the fifteenth and sixteenth centuries (Italian, Byzantine and Russian)

Requirements

wood panel, inside measurements 28cm x 21cm (11" x 8¼")

Matisse Terracotta or Pimento basecoat

Jo Sonja paints:

Red Earth

Napthol Red Light

Yellow Oxide

Black

Burnt Sienna

Ultra Blue Deep

Burgundy

Pale Gold

Warm White

Brushes:

two brushes for applying size and shellac

No 3 round brush

fine liner brush

flat or round brush for basecoating drapery

stylus

transfer paper, white and black (or grey)

gold size – quick dry and water soluble

Schlag metal leaf – 8 to 10 sheets 15cm x 15cm (6" x 6") approximately

shellac for sealing

methylated spirits for cleaning shellac brush

white gloves for handling gold

silk scarf for rubbing gold

Deco Art fine nozzle squeeze bottle and rich gold paint, or gold scribble paint for fabric

Basecoat

Basecoat entire panel and frame and sand lightly. Using the photograph trace the outlines of the design only, do not add details of drapery, facial features or decoration. Trace details onto the haloes. Enlarge to required size and transfer to wood panel.

Basecoat the Madonna's veil in two coats of burgundy and make sure no brushstrokes show. Basecoat the inner veil in Ultra Blue Deep including the sleeve. Ensure no brushstrokes show.

Basecoat Jesus' robes in Napthol Red Light plus Yellow Oxide (1:1).

Basecoat the faces, hands and feet with two coats of Burnt Sienna plus Yellow Oxide plus White or Burnt Sienna plus Napthol Red Light plus Yellow Oxide plus Ultra Blue Deep plus White.

Squeeze or paint the decoration on the haloes in gold. You must leave a ridge or the gold leaf will not look embossed.

Faces

Transfer details onto faces. Study the photograph to check these.

Add White to the skin basecoat and paint highlights onto cheeks, under eyes, along nose, on eyelids and above eyebrows, on chin, blending the edges into the basecoat.

Make up a darker tone by adding less White to the basecoat and paint shadows on the neck, under eyebrows, along nose and under nose, above chin, around cheek, being careful to blend the edges of the shadows into the skin colour.

Lips

Paint a Burnt Sienna line where the lips meet.

The top lip is painted in Burnt Sienna plus Napthol Red Light plus a spot of White.

The lower lip is painted in the same as above plus White with White highlight in centre of lip.

A Burnt Sienna line is painted along the bottom edge of the lower lip.

Eyes

The lid is painted in the light skin colour as above. The outline of the eyes is Black and the iris is painted in Burnt Sienna, while the pupil is Black.

The white of the eye is painted in White plus Napthol Red Light plus Blue plus Yellow (which makes a pale bluish green). Paint a slightly darker shade of this under the eyelid.

The highlight is painted in the same light tone as above.

Hands

These are painted as for Faces above.

Mary's hair

This is painted in Red Earth or Napthol Red plus Yellow Oxide for highlights, Black for shadows and Burnt Sienna for mid tones.

Blue garment

The highlights are painted in Ultra Blue Deep plus White sideload, while the highlights along the top of the sleeve and on neck trim are in Pale Gold.

The large cross pattern is gilded.

Red garment

Highlights are painted in Napthol Red Light sideloaded onto a Burgundy brush. Shadows are painted with Burgundy on the brush and a sideload of Blue.

Jesus' robe

The belt is in Burnt Sienna as is the shoulder decoration and shadow under the arm. Pale Gold is used for the linework.

Trim on Mary's veil

Red Earth plus Yellow Oxide is painted on the highlighted edges blending towards the shadows. The lines are in Rich Gold with highlights of Pale Gold. Tassels are Pale Gold.

Gilding

Paint gold size onto the areas you wish to gild. It is best to work on the frame first as you have only about ten minutes to fiddle with the size before it dries. When the size is tacky put your gloves on and apply the gold leaf, patting it down lightly as you go and overlapping the edges of the gold leaf. If you want a mottled effect, as shown here around the edges of the frame, apply the size in random blotches, allow to dry until tacky and apply the gold leaf.

Paint the background and haloes and crosses in size then gild when tacky, as above.

When all the gold has been patted down, rub with a silk cloth until there are no loose pieces of gold. Seal with shellac.

Antique with oil based patina and Burnt Umber oil paint, applying more intensely around the haloes and frame, especially around the corners.

Ann Johnston

Artist and visual arts teacher, Ann Johnston, a graduate of the National Art School in Sydney, has always had an interest in traditional art forms. Further study in Europe developed her interest in mediaeval, renaissance and pre-Raphaelite art.

Ann has created a unique style of decorative painting, taking inspiration from images throughout history, adapting and transforming them into figuritive, floral and still life designs in acrylics and oils. Most recently Ann has explored further a particular interest in murals, trompe l'oeil painting and faux finishes for domestic and commercial venues.

The four very elegant maidens adorning this little cupboard are an adaptation of a painting by the pre-Raphaelite artist, Edward Burne Jones, called *The Wedding of Psyche* (1894-5). Ann has been inspired by the calm stately aura of this painting, adapting the image and using her own style to recreate her own little piece of history. Burne Jones was one of the most important artists of the second phase of the pre-Raphaelite movement and one of the greatest of all English Romantic painters. Through his lifelong association with William Morris he was also a prolific designer of stained glass, tapestries, tiles, mosaics, books and furniture. His philosophy is summed up in his own definition of a picture as 'a beautiful romantic dream of something that never was, in a light better than any light that ever shone, in a land no one can define or remember, only desire....'

Ann Johnston

Requirements

wood piece to paint – in this case door surfaces measure 36cm wide × 38.5cm high (14'''' × 15")

paints:

Jo Sonja Background Colour Azure

Jo Sonja Artists Gouache:

Burgundy, Burnt Umber, Raw Sienna, Pacific Blue, Rose Pink, Burnt Sienna, Olive Green, Titanium White,

Permanent Alizarin, Raw Umber, Jaune Brilliant

Chroma Archival Oils:

Raw Umber, Paynes Grey, Titanium White, Yellow Oxide, Green Oxide, Raw Sienna, Superchrome Yellow,

Ultramarine Blue, Jaune Brilliant, Burnt Umber, Burnt Sienna, Permanent Orange, Permanent Alizarin,

Sap Green, Olive Green, Pacific Blue, Napthol Crimson

brushes: 2.5cm (1")

background and varnish brush

1.5cm ($^1/_2$") , 7mm ($^1/_4$") and 3mm ($^1/_8$") flat

No 3 round

$^1/_4$" (7mm) filbert

fine liner

small mop brushes, approx 3mm ($^1/_8$") and 7mm ($^1/_4$")

fine sand paper   stylus

tracing paper   transfer paper

oil based varnish   Archival Lean Medium

Archival odourless solvent

Paint the entire surface of your cupboard or chosen piece with two or three coats of Jo Sonja Azure. Sand well between coats. The cabinet can be sanded after the final coat but the area where the image is to be painted could be left, as this will help to create a little 'tooth' for the oil paints to adhere to.

Make a tracing on transparent paper from the pattern and then transfer it to your project piece using whatever colour transparent paper shows the image well. You need not trace all the details at this stage, for example, facial features, folds, flowers can be left, as most areas need to blocked in acrylics first.

Blocking in the image

Using Jo Sonja Artists Gouache and a flat brush suited to the size of the shape, block in the areas as stated below, finishing with a flat opaque surface. (The figures are referred to as 1, 2, 3, 4 moving from left to right.)

Background: the lower section of the background – from the lower tracing line which extends across behind the torsos of the figures. Paint in a mixture of Paynes Grey, Raw Umber plus Titanium White (2:1:2)

All flesh: Create a flesh colour by mixing Titanium White with a little touch of Jaune Brilliant plus a small amount of Raw Sienna and Burnt Sienna to warm the colour.

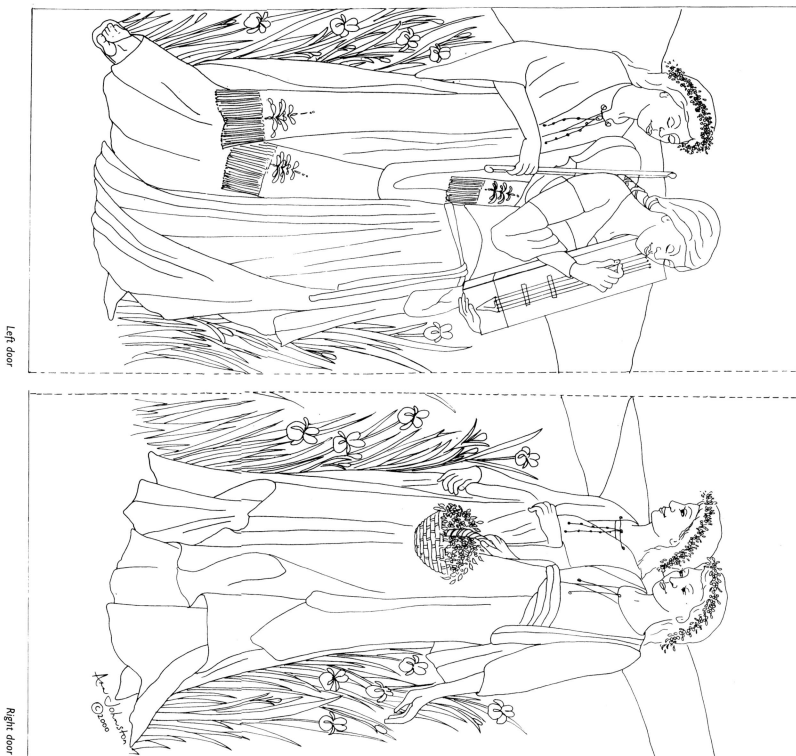

Figure 1.	Dress	Burgundy
	Cape	Raw Sienna
	Hair	Burnt Umber
	Violin	Burnt Umber
	Sandal	Raw Sienna
Figure 2.	Dress	Pacific Blue
	Sash/Armband	Rose Pink plus Burgundy (1:1)
	Hair	Burnt Sienna
	Sandal	Raw Sienna
	Instrument	Burnt Umber
Figure 3.	Dress	Olive Green plus White (1:1)
	Undershirt	Raw Sienna
	Hair	Burnt Umber
Figure 4.	Dress	Burgundy plus Permanent Alizarin (1:1)
	Sash	Raw Umber plus White (1:1)
	Hair	Raw Sienna
	Basket	Raw Sienna

Retrace all detail other than field flowers.

Change to the Archival Oil paints, using the Archival Lean Medium to thin the paint for fine work, for example details on faces, leaves, wreaths, instrument strings.

Background

Paint the background, starting at the top of the painting and moving down either side of the figures. Apply the paint with a 7mm (1/4") flat brush and soften with a mop brush. Mix Paynes Grey plus Titanium White (1:3) and begin brushing in a vertical direction. Approximately halfway down to the next tracing line add more white to the mix, working the two tones together which will give the effect of the sky moving from dark to light. Softly brush over with a mop brush.

The hill behind the figures on the right is painted in Titanium White, Paynes Grey, Yellow Oxide plus Raw Umber (5:2:1:1). Soften the edge where the sky and hill meet, creating a haze effect. The hill on the left which extends over behind the figures on the right (below the hill just completed) is painted by adding a little more Paynes Grey and Raw Umber to the above mix. Work down past the shoulder level. Soften the top edge where the lines meet the above colour. Add more Paynes Grey to the mix (Paynes Grey plus mix 1:1) and work down towards the hemline. The colour should be quite dark.

Add a little Raw Umber to the lower background colour and brush across the foreground.

Faces

The faces are all painted in a similar manner. Mix Titanium White with a little Jaune Brilliant plus a small touch of Raw Sienna and Burnt Sienna. Take a small amount of this mix and add a little Burnt Sienna and Burnt Umber (1:1:1). This deeper tone will be used for all shadows on the flesh and the lighter as the main flesh colour. Paint the irises which can be seen in Burnt Umber. Place a little white highlight off centre. Refer to the photograph and paint on the shadows of the face using the deeper flesh tone in the area that extends from the corner of the eye nearest to the nose and over the eyelid. Extend the shadow down the side of the nose and lower lip and under the chin and as appropriate on the neck. A little can be brushed against the hairline and inside the ear and around the lobe of the ear. Fill all other areas on the face with the pale flesh colour (do not blend together at this stage). Do not apply too much paint, rather 'stretch' the paint so the application is smooth. Using a small mop brush lightly brush over the face blending the two tones together. Do not over blend, so the paint will stay fresh.

Check to see if the darker tones need to be reinforced with a little extra paint. Add a little Titanium White to the paler tone and lay down a few added highlights such as on the eyelids, under the eyebrow, the top of the nose, chin, lobe of the ear, and so on. Soften with a little mop brush. Paint the eyebrows with a liner brush in Burnt Sienna. Paint a Burnt Umber line along the top and bottom lid to represent the eyelashes and a line between the lips. The lips are painted in Napthol Crimson plus a touch of Burnt Sienna. Add a little White to the mix and place highlights through the centre of the top and bottom lip. Touch a little of the same colour on the cheeks and tap out with a mop brush to create a soft finish.

Arms and hands

The arms and hands are treated in a similar manner to the faces. Begin by laying down the darkest tone followed by the lighter and blend softly with a mop brush. Details such as fingernails can be painted with a liner brush. (Do not over emphasise.) Paint the foot on the left in a similar manner.

Hair

Figure 1. Mix Burnt Umber into a little Lean Medium and brush over the hair area. Mix Burnt Sienna plus Raw Sienna (1:1) and build up strands of hair with a liner brush. A little White can be added to the mix for extra highlights. The leaves in the wreath are painted in Green Oxide plus Sap Green (1:1). Add lighter leaves on top in straight Sap Green. The flowers are tiny daisies painted in Yellow Oxide plus White (1:2).

Figure 2. Mix Burnt Sienna into a little Lean Medium and brush on. Follow this with a mix of Burnt Sienna, Raw Sienna plus White (2:2:1) and brush on with a 7mm (1/4") filbert brush allowing some of the dark tone to show. Add White to the mid tone for added highlights. Paint the ribbon Napthol Crimson plus a touch of White.

Figure 3. Base as above in Burnt Umber and Lean Medium followed by Burnt Umber plus White for the highlights, painted on with a liner brush. Small wisps of hair are painted around the hairline and down the nape of the neck. The wreath leaves are painted the same as for Figure 1 followed by little Titanium White daisies.

Figure 4. Base in Raw Sienna plus Lean Medium followed by Raw Sienna plus White highlights applied with a 7mm (1/4") filbert, allowing the deeper tone to show through. The leaves in the wreath are painted in Burnt Sienna followed by Permanent Alizarin berries. Add an occasional Superchrome Yellow one.

Garments

The garments are each painted the same way. Using a 7mm ($^1/_4"$) flat or filbert brush, and the photograph as a guide, lay down the deepest tone first, followed by mid tone. Do not use too much paint, simply place the tones side by side and meld them together with the same brush. The lightest tone is then placed on the mid tone where appropriate (where more light is showing) and lightly blended. The whole garment is then softly blended by a light over brushing with a mop brush. Do not overblend. The cord at the neck is painted in Raw Sienna plus White. The depth of the fold is created by strong contrasts in tone. Too much blending will flatten the folds and overwork the paint.

Figure 1

Undergarment:

deep tone	Alizarin Crimson plus Burnt Umber (3:1)
mid tone	Alizarin Crimson plus Permanent Orange (4:1)
light tone	mid tone plus a touch of White

The cord at the neck is painted in Raw Sienna plus White

Overgarment:

deep tone	Raw Sienna plus Burnt Sienna (1:1)
mid tone	Raw Sienna plus White (1:1)
light tone	add more white to the mid tone

The pattern on the edge of the stole is painted in Raw Sienna plus Burnt Sienna (1:1) and the fringe in Raw Sienna and White.

The sandal is painted in Raw Sienna followed by Burnt Sienna plus White (1:1) highlights and outlined in Burnt Sienna.

Figure 2

Blue area:

deep tone	Pacific Blue plus Paynes Grey (1:1)
mid tone	Pacific Blue
light tone	Pacific Blue plus White (1:1)

Pink area:

deep tone	Napthol Crimson
mid tone	Napthol Crimson plus White (1:1)
light tone	Napthol Crimson plus White (1:2)

The shoe is painted in Raw Sienna plus White (1:1)

Figure 3

Undergarment:

dark tone	Raw Sienna
mid tone	Raw Sienna plus White (1:1)
light tone	Raw Sienna plus White (2:1)

Overgarment:

dark tone	Olive Green
mid tone	Olive Green plus White (1:1)
light tone	Olive Green plus White (1:2)

The tie at the neck is painted in Burnt Umber.

Figure 4

Dress:

dark tone	Permanent Alizarin plus a touch of Burnt Umber
mid tone	Permanent Alizarin plus White (2:1)
light tone	Permanent Alizarin plus White (1:1)

Sash:

dark tone	Raw Umber plus White (1:1)
light tone	Raw Umber plus White (1:3)

The tie at the neck is Permanent Alizarin. The shoe is Burnt Sienna plus Raw Sienna (2:1). Add a touch of White for the highlights.

Basket: Mix Raw Sienna plus Lean Medium and brush over the basket. Basketweave Raw Sienna plus White (1:1) around the basket and paint fine Burnt Sienna lines here and there on the side of some of the Raw Sienna strokes.

The leaves in the basket are Green Oxide plus Titanium White and the flowers are painted in Permanent Alizarin plus White, mixed on the brush to allow variations in tone. Dot the centres in Raw Sienna plus White.

Instruments

Violin: Base in Burnt Umber plus Lean Medium. Brush over in Burnt Sienna leaving the Burnt Umber around the edges. Add Titanium White to the Burnt Sienna and brush on highlights on the side. Use this colour mix for the bow. The strings are painted in Raw Sienna plus Titanium White.

Zither: Base in Burnt Umber plus Lean Medium. Mix Burnt Sienna plus Raw Sienna and brush on, leaving the edges, bridges and lower sections of the instruments in Burnt Umber. Add a little Titanium White to the mix and highlight the side. The strings are painted in Raw Sienna plus White.

Field flowers

The leaves are painted in long strokes using a No 3 round brush. Add a touch of Lean Medium to the paint.

Dark colour: Paynes Grey

Mid colour: Green Oxide plus Sap Green (1:1) (Paint fewer of these.)

The flowers are painted with 4mm (1/8") flat brush.

Blue flowers

Paint the petals first in Paynes Grey and then overlay by gently placing a mix of Ultramarine Blue plus Pacific Blue plus Titanium White (2:1:1) allowing some of the Paynes Grey to show. Pick up a bit of Yellow Oxide followed by Superchrome Yellow on a liner brush and paint the centre. Paint a blue bud here and there.

White flowers

Paint in a similar manner to the blue flowers, beginning with Raw Sienna and overlaying in Titanium White. Paint the occasional Titanium White bud.

Finishing

Allow several weeks for your project to dry in a dust free environment before finishing with two coats of oil based varnish.

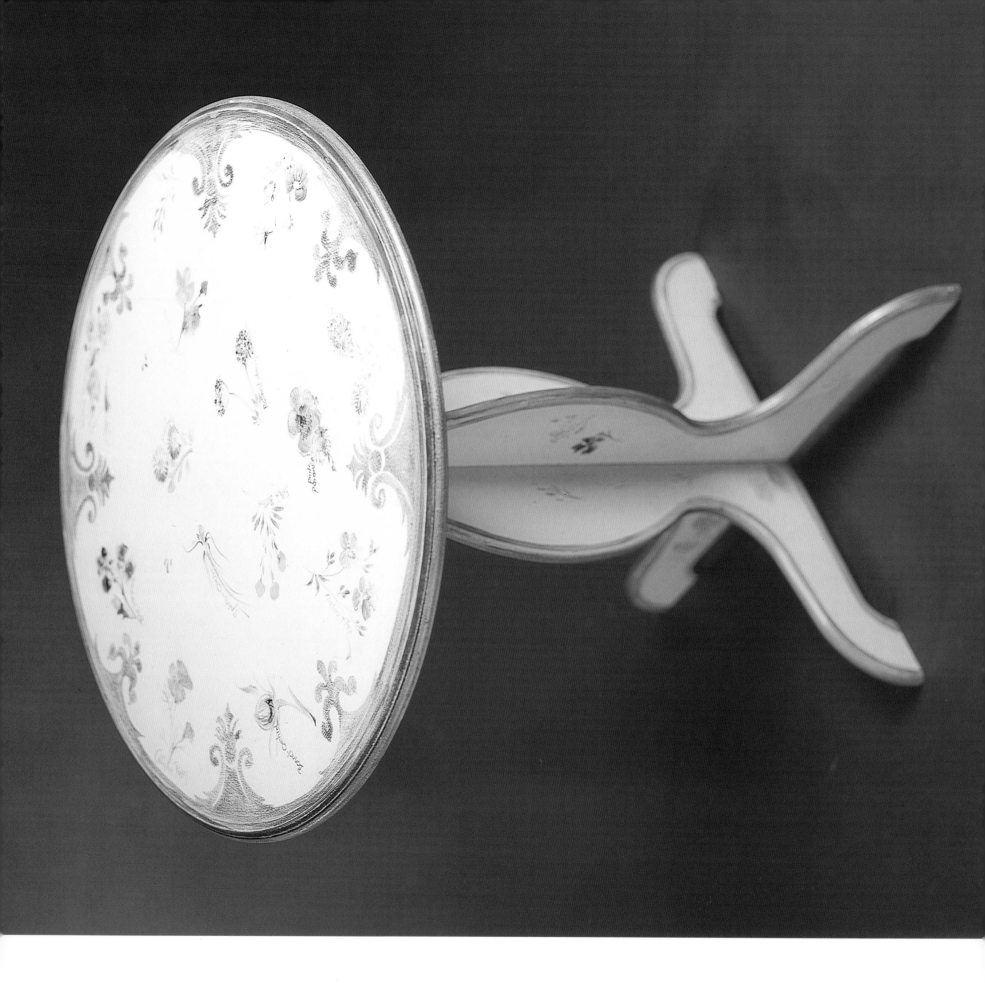

Jane Devine

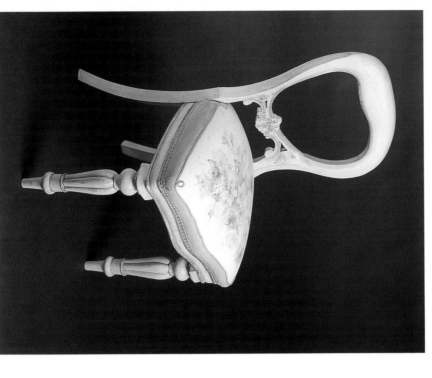

Watercolour painting is Jane Devine's first love, and she exhibits every two or three years with great success. However, while living in Europe for several years she became fascinated by painted furniture. Returning to Australia, she began painting and decorating wooden pieces and ran many 'workshops, spreading her enthusiasm to others.

Painted furniture is one of the oldest crafts. Wonderful examples have been found dating as far back as 1600BC. From the simplest farmhouse pieces to the most elaborate baroque masterpieces, furniture has been decorated for centuries. These pieces are highly adaptable and highly collectable.

Jane's inspiration is the piece of furniture itself — its shape and size determine the type of design she applies. She is, of course, adamant that fine antiques should never be painted, no matter how tempting, but rather reproductions, or furniture which requires heavy lacquering anyway. If they need to be sealed and stained in this way, then why not paint them?

Not one to limit herself to wooden surfaces, Jane also likes to paint on the cloth seats of chairs. This is an alternative to the tapestry upholstery which is so admired, but so time consuming.

Jane is a talented watercolourist and illustrator, but her training as an art teacher allows her to pass on many of her techniques to others, encouraging them to be creative and adventurous in their work.

Far left: A little extra table 60cm (24") high, 50cm (20") diameter

Left: Bedroom chair 90cm (36") high, seat 48cm (19") wide, 38cm (15") deep

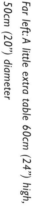

Jane Devine

Sewing Table

Requirements

gesso or sealer/undercoat
basecoat Moss Green
Jo Sonja's Artists' Acrylic paints:

Ultramarine Deep
Dioxazine Purple
Burgundy
Yellow Oxide
White
Green Oxide
Burnt Umber

butchers paper and pencil
plastic cling wrap
gilding kit (optional)
Estapol sealer
brushes

You might not have a table of this shape, in which case, adapt the border design to suit the table you do have. This border is approximately 7.5cm (3") wide. For a larger table, make it proportionately wider. The choice of flowers is personal. Because Jane wanted the table to be 'dirty green', the three colours she likes to go with this green are blues, pinks and creams. Therefore the choice of flowers then became easier. Morning glory was an obvious choice, especially as the shape of the flower is angular, as is the table. Cream lilies are simple in shape and Jane thought 'fluffy', complicated flowers such as full blown roses would not suit the shape, so she chose simple, open roses.

Paint the table with sealer/undercoat. This will show the imperfections. Fill any major gaps but leave minor imperfections. Dry and sand lightly.

Take a piece of butchers paper and mark the exact size of the table top. Draw in a border strip approximately 7.5cm (3") wide, or to your own size. Enlarge the design on the next page to size either in pieces or on an extra large photocopier. Then arrange the enlarged pieces onto your butchers paper shape adding and subtracting to fit. (If you wish to use other flowers, select them from the garden, stick them onto a piece of white paper with clear tape, turn the paper face down on the photocopier, and there you have your own flower outlines. Take each flower one at a time and trace them at regular intervals around the border.)

Paint all the border first. Take one flower variety at a time and fill them all in with a fairly watery wash. While still wet, drop a dot into the centre, generally Yellow Oxide or Green. Move on to the next flower variety and repeat this process. Then paint all the leaves. Use some colour variation for each, adding a little blue to the morning glory leaves and a little yellow to the lily leaves. Allow to dry well.

The next flower coat is a similar wash, but not over the entire flower. Add a swish of a very similar colour across one or two of the petals to give form and depth. Shadows can be added with watery Dioxazine Purple, or a dash of Burnt Umber will do as well. Dry well.

Sewing table 60cm (24") high, 40cm (16") across, 18cm (7") each side

Gilded floral frame 68cm x 78cm (27" x 31")

Sue Trytell

The art and craft of gilding has been practised for thousands of years. The Egyptians applied gold leaf freely to statues, mummy casks, coffins and other items of funerary equipment. Beaten gold leaf can be dated back to 2000BC in the Andes of Southern Peru. In Europe, gilding was used extensively in the Renaissance, Baroque and Rococo periods to adorn furniture such as tables, chairs, picture and mirror frames. Icons, picture frames and art work heavily gilded with genuine gold still adorn temples and places of worship all over the world.

Sue Trytell is an accomplished and experienced gilder who uses this traditional craft in different and highly decorative ways. A self confessed 'Bower Bird' Sue loves nothing more than transforming every day objects into the extraordinary. Sue's philosophy is not to discard unwanted items but, rather to use her imagination and creative adornment to bring about a rebirth.

Constantly experimenting and working in new fields, here Sue combines gold leaf with dried flowers to create a lavish mirror frame.

The finished frame is 68cm × 78cm (27" × 31") and the mirror frame is 24cm × 40cm ($9^1/_2$" × $15^3/_4$"). The work looks best if hung vertically.

You can purchase gilded frames for this mirror, however below are Sue's instructions for gilding the frames should you so desire.

Sue Trytell

Jennifer Bennell

Decorative paint finishes and the name of Jennifer Bennell are almost synonymous. Jennifer has maintained and continued a tradition spanning centuries, while exploring new techniques and materials.

Jennifer studied at the Gale Laurence, Joanne Day Studio in San Francisco, completing most of the courses on offer at the time. These teachers had achieved some fame when working for Isabel O'Neil in her New York studio before moving to the west coast. Isabel O'Neil had been almost solely responsible for the re-introduction of decorative paint finishes into the United States of America, offering these complicated and difficult finishes in a simpler and more readily achievable manner.

Upon her return to Australia, Jennifer set up her studio, The Painted Finish, in 1984. In the following years she trained thousands of students, many of whom went on to become sought-after specialist paint finishers both in Australia and abroad. Her studio offered training in every facet of paint finishes and included all aspects of preparation for restoration.

Among the techniques Jennifer taught were: faux marbling, Japanese lacquer, faux skin, tortoiseshell, oil-gilding and water-gilding, as well as reverse gilding and painting on glass. New and innovative paints developed by Jennifer were also introduced. These included real copper and real iron paints which oxidise to verdigris and rust respectively with the application of an oxidant.

During this time, as well as training others, Jennifer ran a large, commercial, decorative paint finish business, completing finishes in many public and corporate buildings, both in Australia and overseas, as well as in private residences.

Jennifer sold the name, The Painted Finish, in 1996 and now concentrates on the manufacture, marketing and distribution of her range of paints, Magic Effects.

Distressed finish cupboard and stool

Distressed-finish cupboard

Note: this cupboard was built by Jennifer Bennell at cabinetmaking classes. Any cupboard with a raw wood finish could be treated in this way, or you could have a cupboard made for you.

Requirements – Fabric lining

white cotton fabric to fit internal doors and walls of cupboard

Magic Effects:

Real Copper Paint	ruler
Oxidising Patina	45° level
	stencil
narrow crepe masking tape	pencil
various flat acrylic household paints	

A trellis pattern is marked onto the fabric. The scale of the trellis really depends on the size of the cupboard and the fabric showing through. In this case the 'wood' strips are 5mm wide and the 'space' between is 4.5cm.

Using the 45° level and measuring up from the centre and down from the centre of your fabric, mark the first piece of trellis, in one direction only. Then, working out from the centre, mark both edges of each piece of trellis, in one direction only, with a pencil and ruler. Then apply crepe masking tape to both edges of each piece of one way trellis. Run a thumbnail carefully along the edges of the tape so your paint does not seep under. This is especially important with taped fabric.

Paint the negative space between the strips of tape with Real Copper Paint (this dries almost immediately when applied to fabric). Paint the Oxidising Patina over the dried Copper Paint and this will turn almost immediately to verdigris. Allow a little copper to show through.

Remove the masking tape and draw in and then mask the cross members of the trellis. Apply the Oxidising Patina and Copper Paint in the same way.

The stencil Jennifer has used here is a *Passiflora edulis* five part design. It has been painted on with flat household acrylic paint.

Staple the fabric to the inside of the doors, sides and back of the cupboard.

Requirements – Distressed finish

Magic Effects:	Special Paint – Alchemy
	Special Paint – Bedazzled
	Heavy Duty Varnish (satin or gloss) if necessary
5cm (2") good quality nylon paint brush	220 garnet sandpaper
1200 wet and dry sandpaper	tack rag
cotton rags	

This plaster-based paint acts as a sealer/undercoat. Apply one coat of Alchemy (green) to the raw wood. Allow to dry for approximately 30 minutes, but this will depend upon the weather.

Sand thoroughly with the 220 garnet. In doing so you will feel the wood become smooth and at the same time you will be distressing the paint finish. You will find you are removing paint from areas which would normally receive wear, and therefore the distressing is quite realistic. Dust off all sanding residue.

Thin one part Bedazzled (blue) with three parts water. Apply to the green background and wipe into the finish with a dry cotton cloth. The paint will be absorbed into the green background and will dry almost immediately. If the blue is not strong enough, simply re-apply.

To finish lightly sand with dry 1200 wet and dry sandpaper. This gives a very smooth finish without removing the paint. Jennifer prefers to leave this finish as is, however, for protection apply two coats of varnish, or wax (which does not have the same protective qualities as varnish).

Stool

This stool has a four colour distressed finish applied to the seats and steps. The rest of the stool is in a solid colour from the range of colours used on the seats and steps. Varnish has been applied to the seat and steps only.

Requirements

5cm (2") good quality nylon brush

tack rag

Magic Effects: Special Paint – White, Bedazzled, Alchemy, Sorcerer

Heavy Duty Varnish, satin or gloss

220 garnet sandpaper

cotton rags

Clean and sand the surface, dust and then apply one coat of white paint. This paint is plaster-based and is very quick drying and acts as a sealer for raw materials.

Have your four colours open at once. (See sample board 1.)

When dry (after approximately 30 minutes, depending on the weather), sand and dust off.

Load the brush with one colour, take off some on a piece of paper, then, holding the brush side on to the surface, roughly brush the paint onto the white surface, covering about 25 per cent with colour, leaving about 75 per cent uncovered by paint and still white. Because of the plaster base of these paints the white and coloured paints are very absorbent and will start to dry immediately. Wipe the brush with a rag to remove any excess colour and dip brush into the next colour, again covering another 25 per cent of the whole surface. (See sample board 2.)

Repeat this process with the third and fourth colours so the white background is no longer apparent.

Wipe the brush, then use it to blend the colours slightly together. If the paint is too dry to blend, soften a cloth with water and work over the surface and you will find the colours blend quite readily. Or dampen the brush with water and it will work equally well.

When the surface is dry, apply two coats of varnish for protection, or wax (although this is not as protective as varnish).

Note: You might wish one colour to predominate. If so cover 50 – 75 per cent of the surface with that colour and then work in the other colours. If you want a more distressed look, sand back to reveal some white.

Sample board 1 showing one coat of white and samples of each of the four colours used on the stool

Sample board 2 showing blue applied roughly followed by green applied roughly. Note the white still showing through

Sample board 3 showing pink applied roughly followed by yellow applied roughly so that the white background is completely covered

Sample board 4 showing all colours blended again roughly to give an impression of distressing

Dining system, Japanese Embassy, Canberra. Returns for separated round tables are hidden in semi-circular bases of full table, and they featur

Furniture

David Upfill-Brown

S culptor turned furniture maker, David Upfill-Brown reveals his past experiences in his present work. David's furniture exhibits the fluid, curved lines of a sculptor, combined with the precision in jointing required for the structural integrity of his pieces.

David developed his interest in sculpture while working with the Shona sculptors in Zimbabwe and became a successful sculptor himself, working in South Africa for a number of years. Moving to England, he widened and refined his skills at the John Makepeace School for Craftsmen in Wood in Dorset. He has made an extensive study of different timbers and their properties and his involvement with a timber agency in Australia allowed him greater access to and knowledge of high quality Australian timber.

In Australia, David worked for many years on production pieces but in recent years he has achieved great success with his commission work, not only for private clients, but creating important pieces for public and corporate institutions, such as the parliaments of Australia, Papua New Guinea, the Marshall Islands and the Solomon Islands, along with many more. One of the most recent is the 'dining system' shown here, made for the Japanese Embassy in Canberra, Australia. Echoing the Japanese shoji, or panels, it has the ability to be assembled as one large table or many smaller tables, requiring the complex design solution of a hidden return for the round tables, as well as meticulous attention to detail in the perfectly fitted removable leaves and falling leaf or flip top.

For many years David has combined his commission work with his teaching of adults, both at his own, large workshop and at the Canberra Institute of the Arts. Now he is Academic Director of the Australian School of Fine Furniture Ltd, a new initiative in Tasmania, Australia.

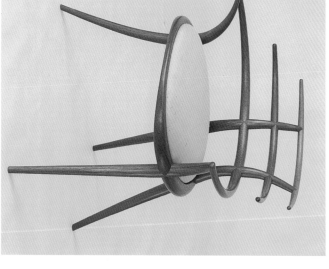

One of a pair of chair in laminated jarrah with oiled finish

David Upfill-Brown

Dining System, Japanese Embassy, Canberra, blackwood, with fibreglass shoji panels, with plastic finish, designed for a variable number of diners, made with Andrew Tarnawsky.

Right: Conversation piece in Queensland silver ash, laminated, carved legs and oiled finish.

Japanese table – gluing assembled pieces – Andrew Tarnawsky tuning the sliding returns.

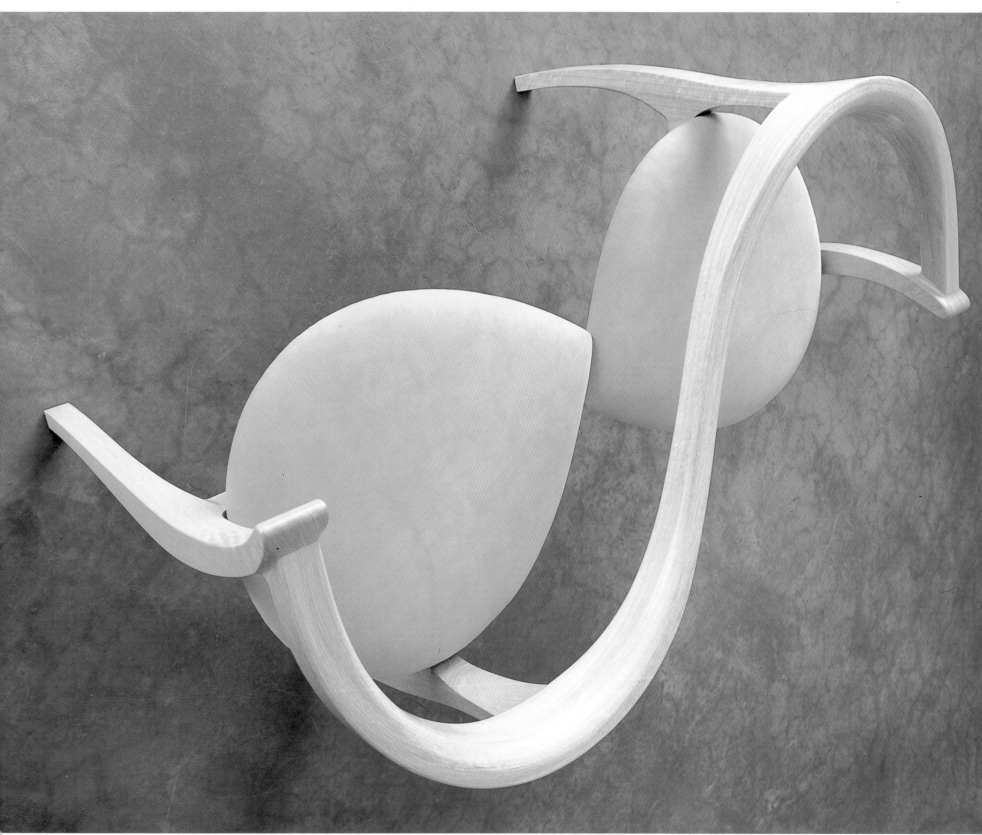

Richard Raffan

Richard Raffan began turning wood in January 1970 at the age of 26, moving on from a successful career in the London wine trade. He has earned his living from the craft ever since. In 1982 he emigrated to Australia where he has extensive family connections.

In June 1970, after four months training in a small production workshop, Richard established his own studio and started to refine his basic lathe skills. For some years he developed techniques while turning standard production bowls, platters, boxes, and scoops, as well as components for the joinery and furniture trades. At the same time he created a market in the then new craft galleries for fine turning and particularly for 'one off' decorative bowls.

In 1973 Richard was the only woodturner represented in the seminal exhibition *The Craftsman's Art* at the Victoria and Albert Museum in London, and this quickly established him as a leading figure in the hand crafts revival: since then his work has been acquired for public and private collections across the world. He has been a major influence on a generation of woodturners worldwide, both technically and artistically. Since 1980, Richard has been in demand as an educator and demonstrator in North America, Europe and Australasia but, with orders to meet and galleries to supply, he limits his teaching to just a few weeks each year. He is well known for his articles, reviews, videos, and four books: *Turning Wood*, *Turned Bowl Design*, *Turning Projects* and *Turning Boxes*. The first two are widely regarded as woodturning classics.

Today Richard's main interest is the creation of individual objects or groups of objects for collectors, which stand alongside his fine, gallery quality, utilitarian bowls. He insists his bowls are designed to be used. If kept dry they can be wax polished and soon develop an antique patina. Or they can be used for food and hand washed in hot water with detergent.

From a tonne of carefully cut timber Richard reckons to obtain about 200 medium size salad bowls and up to twice the number of much smaller bowls, depending on the species of wood. As a professional woodturner specialising in bowls he purchases wood while it is still 'green' or unseasoned. This is partly because dry wood of the dimensions he requires is virtually unobtainable, but mostly because the wood is easier to work when green. Like many woodturners, by working unseasoned wood, Richard can use parts of trees other woodworkers, who need seasoned wood, would regard as unusable.

River red gum bowl
27cm x 12cm
(10 1/2" x 4 3/4")

Eucalypt burl wavy bowls (left)
15cm x 5cm
(6" x 2"); 12cm x 4cm (4 3/4" x 1 1/2"); 12.5cm x 4cm
(5" x 1 1/2")

Richard Raffan

Gidgee bowl with bark rim 19cm x 11cm (7¹/₂" x 4¹/₄")

The traditional rule of thumb for seasoning timber is a year per inch (2.5cm) of thickness, plus a year. Thus a solid block of wood for a typical salad bowl would require seasoning for at least five years. Clearly this would be impractical: for a start any professional would need heaps of space to store five or six years' worth of raw material. This would tie up capital for an asset which is sure to degrade through splitting as it dries, and which is likely to be attacked by termites and coring insects. So professional bowl turners partly turn bowls for seasoning and reduce the seasoning time to a matter of months, or two years at the most.

Richard purchases most of his wood by the pallet load from timber dealers who cut it to his requirements in the forest then ship it to him on pallets. The moment the freshly felled wood arrives at his workshop, he transforms it into roughly shaped bowls which will be set aside to season and warp. Once dry, the rough bowls are remounted on the lathe for completion.

Richard begins to turn his bowls by cutting round blanks on his bandsaw, keeping larger off-cuts for small bowls. These are much easier to work when seasoned.

The centre of the bowls used to be wasted as shavings, but specialised tools now enable woodturners like Richard to extract further bowls from the original blank.

The rough turned bowls are dated, then left to dry, out of the direct sun where air can circulate round them. After a few weeks' drying they are transferred into large boxes, and there they stay for one to two years.

Richard explains 'there are methods of forcing the seasoning process using kilns, but the structure of the timber changes and the wood never works as well as if air dried. The longer wood can season naturally the better it gets. I've been lucky enough to work wood known to be hundreds of years old and it's a magical experience, so the longer I can leave my wood seasoning, the better.'

Once dry, the part turned bowls are remounted on the lathe for completion. First, the form is refined using gouges and scrapers, then sanded. Finally, oil is applied and allowed to soak into the wood before a layer of beeswax is applied and polished.

Richard often turns bowls using freshly felled wood, knowing they will warp as they dry. The bowls are turned like any other, but because the wood is wet and turned very thin, they demand exceptional skill. The smaller bowls are dried in a microwave oven in a few minutes. Bowls too large for the microwave take about six months to stabilise. Richard explains this method of working: 'I need to get just the right sort of wood. It has to be even grained and a species which warps dramatically. By aligning the grain carefully in the blank, and through careful shaping, I can pretty much predict the final form.'

Forest she-oak bowl (as shown in photographs of Richard working) 19.5cm x 6cm (7 3/4" x 2 1/4") with Jarrah burl wavy bowl 12cm x 5cm (4 3/4" x 2")

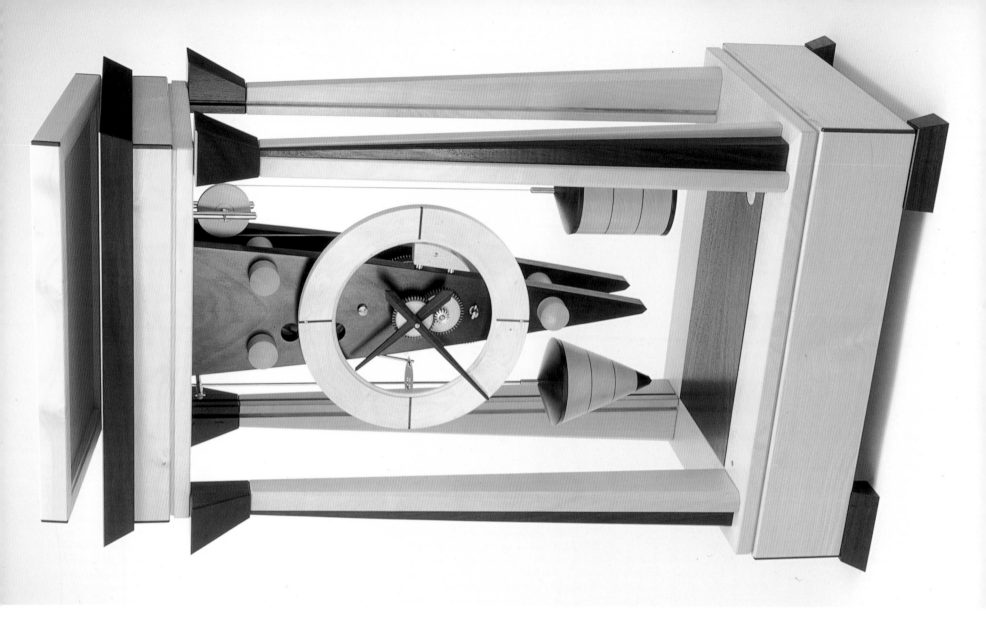

860mm high x 480mm wide x
270mm deep
satin box, ancient redgum, brass,
stainless steel, high density
fibreboard

William Matthysen

The timepieces of Will Matthysen are mounted in simple glass cabinets, some with additional architectural details, such as columns, capitals and cornices. They combine traditional woodworking skills such as turning and joinery with the intricate and precision engineering of clockmaking. An experienced architect, trained in South Africa and England, Will studied woodworking and later watch and clockmaking part time in Victoria. He has been making clocks for almost ten years. He finds one of the joys of clockmaking is that it requires attention to detail at every step. There is simply no way to cut corners.

The use of wood in clockmaking is not new. The Swiss and Black Forest Germans used wood in the seventeenth century, and the Americans mass produced wooden clocks in the early nineteenth century.

Like these earlier clockmakers, Will Matthysen uses other materials such as steel and brass for the pivots and bushes. The teeth of the wheels are either of timber or high density fibreboards for the smaller sized clocks. The clock plates are generally of native Australian hardwood, finished to reveal the natural beauty of the timber.

Timber is quite suitable for clockmaking, as the loads are relatively light, however what is important is the dimensional stability of the wood. Will tries to arrange dimensionally critical parts parallel to the grain and quarter cut timber is essential, preferably from species with a low shrinkage coefficient.

Will normally re-saws his timber soon after purchase and racks it out in the loft space of his workshop. During the summer months temperatures there reach 30° – 40°C (86°F – 104°F), with relative humidity of 60 – 65 per cent. The moisture content of the timber stored in this way is around 10 per cent.

This timber is then re-sawn into blank sizes for the various components and dried further. This is done in Will's home made drying cabinet, which consists of a large cardboard box, with wire mesh shelves to support the blanks, and one or two light bulbs at the bottom (at least 15cm, 6" from the cardboard) to an 8 per cent moisture content.

This wood is then racked out in the workshop to allow it to rehydrate and stabilise in workshop conditions. Will carries out a final check on moisture content before machining and laminating.

With the exception of a few grub screws, Will makes all the parts for the clocks in his workshop. He makes many of the manufactured components, such as wheels, pinions, ratchets and arbors, in batches, 50 to a 100 of each. He spends time setting

Will Matthysen

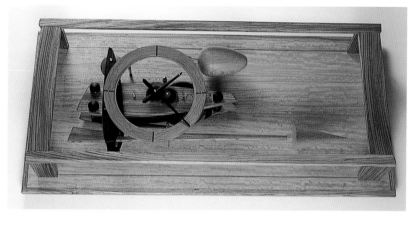

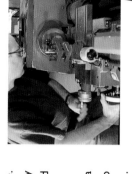

I.

up the machine, test runs it, makes adjustments and perfects his techniques.

Once the machining is complete, he begins the assembly and finds it is always essential to allow for some adjustments in the way the components come together. The brass bushes are friction-fitted into the wooden clock plates and can be adjusted to provide sufficient 'end shake' for the wheels. Likewise, the depth of mesh of the wheels and pinions, and escapement, is achieved by fractionally rotating an eccentric bush.

Once these adjustments are made, the pendulum is begun. This consists of two parts, the rod and the bob. The stability of rod length is critical to the timekeeping performance of the clock. This is where wood is ideally suited. For example, a pendulum rod made from blackwood 1 metre (40") long, will vary in length between summer and winter by 0.125mm. Steel would change by twice as much, and brass by three times that amount. Wood seems ideal as Will's long case clocks run to an accuracy of within a minute a week.

Now he mounts the movement onto a temporary board. A tin can filled with lead weights is hooked to the winding barrel, and he starts the pendulum moving slightly. It should spring to life itself. While he test runs the workings for a few weeks he has time to make the clock case. During this time the pendulum, originally made overlength, is progressively shortened until it is within timekeeping range.

The pendulum bob is then added. This is a turned wooden shape which is attached to the pendulum by means of a threaded rod. This allows for finetuning of the clock. A driving weight is added to the other side. Will cores it out and fills it with the correct amount of lead. He initially runs the clock with a weight just sufficient to keep it ticking over, and then adds 50 per cent. This

1570mm high x 480mm wide x
235mm deep
zebrano, ebony, satin box, brass,
stainless steel, high density fibreboard

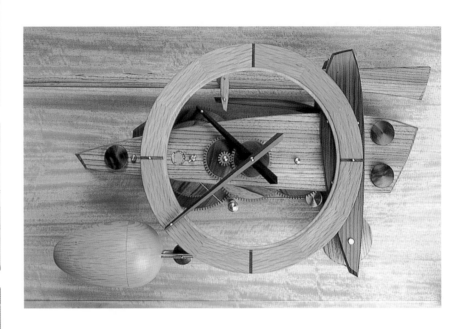

allows for any increase in friction due to dirt or dust which might accumulate over time. Fractionally adjusting the length of the pendulum by turning the bob speeds up or slows down the workings. Raising the bob will make the mechanism work faster and vice versa.

The whole movement is then run for about a month while final adjustments are made, then it is cleaned and oiled and assembled within its case.

Detail left.

1400mm high x 680mm wide x 210mm deep

zebrano, ebony, rose sheoak, brass, stainless steel, high density fibreboard

1. Truing up some wheel blanks on the lathe

2. Machining a batch of wheel blanks on the milling machine. The compound table traverses the rotating cutter from left to right. The rotary table with the indexing plate is rotated to a tooth width before commencing the next cut

3. A home made depthing tool is used to check the mesh of a wheel and pinion. The depth of mesh is critical and ensures the smooth running of the wheel train. The distance between centres is then directly transferred to the clock plates

4. Polishing the pivots. Pivots are made from hardened steel and polished to a mirror finish to minimise friction

5. Drilling and boring the centre hole of a complete wheel. The woodturning chuck has been adapted for use on the metal lathe. The chuck has been fitted with medium density fibreboard 'soft jaws' which have been turned with a rebate to suit the wheel diameter. The wheel can now be accurately centred and drilled

6. The completed wheel assemblies are assembled on the clock plates

7. The top clock plate and dial are fitted.

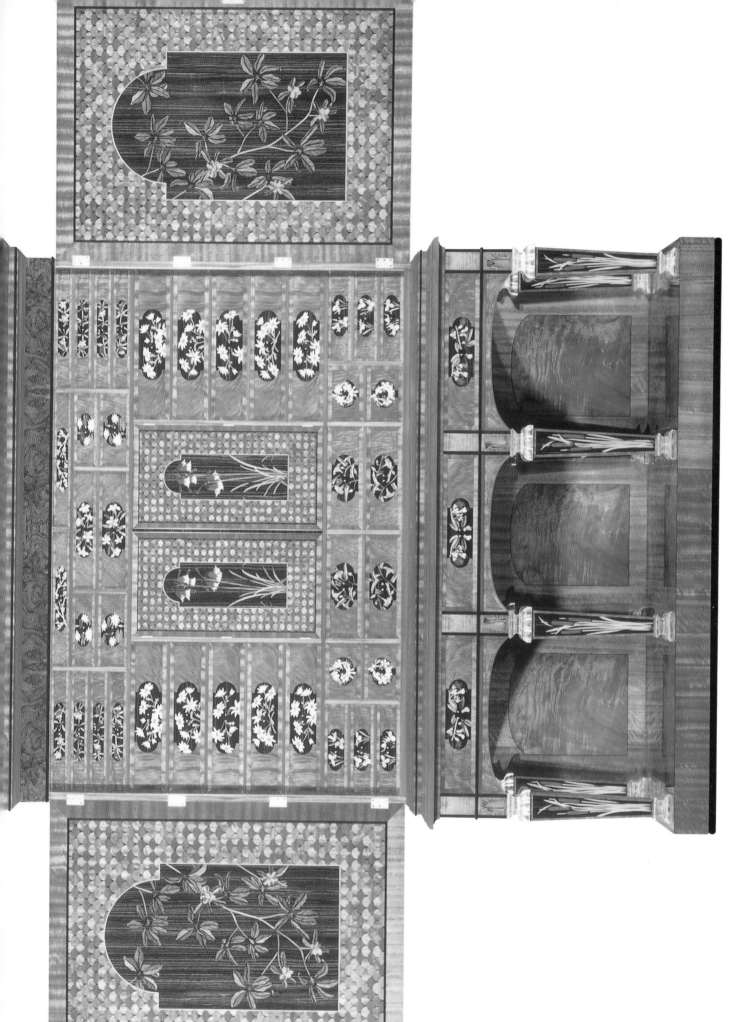

Geoffrey Hannah

One of the most enthusiastic and energetic of all woodworkers, Geoffrey Hannah is also one of the most skilled. Apprenticed as a cabinet maker at 15, today his pieces are held in several collections in Australia, including the residence of the Governor General and in private collections in many other countries.

In 1980 Geoff was awarded a Churchill Fellowship and travelled through England and France researching fine furniture from 1635 – 1850. He won the Traditional Furniture Section of the National Woodwork Exhibition in Melbourne for many years.

Geoff travels throughout Australia conducting workshops in furniture making, marquetry and restoration techniques. His classes are much sought after as his dedication and enthusiasm for his craft is infectious and he is able to explain techniques simply and practically.

The Australian Collectors' Cabinet shown here is one of Geoff's greatest achievements. It took him two years to complete using 100 different types of timber and veneer, of which 90 are native to Australia. The cabinet shows the depth of his knowledge of Australian woods and other timbers, as well as his love for Australian wildflowers. The two main doors feature exquisite marquetry of the floral emblems of each Australian state and territory. Each corner depicts rock isotome, the centre top and bottom shows *Phebalium notti*, while the centre side panels show mountain correa. The drawers are inlaid with black bean flowers and the legs, gilded top and bottom, are inlaid with petrified wood at the top with bull rushes down the length.

The cabinet opens to reveal doors featuring marquetry of Christmas bells (centre) and *Pittosporum revolotum* (interiors of main doors). The drawers depict emu bush, wattle, majestic white waterlily, sweet apple berry, flannel flowers, yellow iris, scrub daphne and swamp convolvulus.

The centre doors open through three more layers to reveal still more detailed marquetry, not only on the insides and outsides of doors, but on drawer fronts and even knobs. In all, there are 100 drawers.

Australiana Collectors' Cabinet
215cm high x 170cm long x 53cm deep (7' 1 3/4" x 5' 7 1/2" x 1' 11")

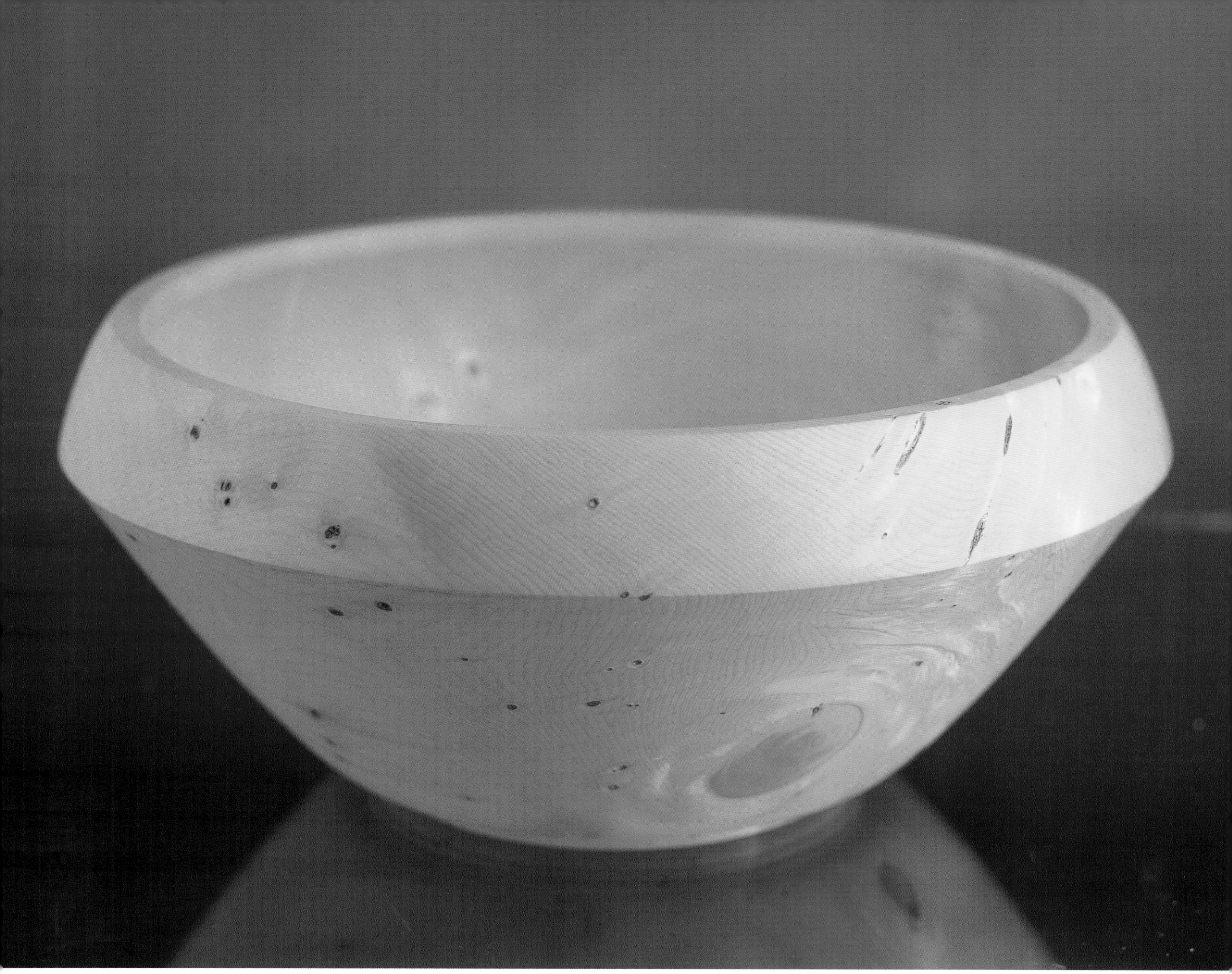

Huon pine bowl 25cm high x 30cm diameter (10" x 12")

Adrian Hunt

Escapees from Australia's largest city, Adrian Hunt and his family set up a woodworking/tourism venture in Tasmania 16 years ago. While this is the dream of many, seldom does it prove such a success. Adrian Hunt is nearly always at his lathe, demonstrating as he works, and his output of fine turnings reaches a ready market. He works entirely in south-west Tasmanian timbers, using simple good design and natural finishes. Adrian's skill and eye for aesthetically drawing the heart of a piece of wood into a functional or decorative work continues to develop. The bowl shown here, made from one of the rarest timbers in Australia, if not the world, is one example of this.

Huon pine bowl

Adrian explains the source of his wood: 'The tree from which this bowl came, grew on a bank of the Huon River in southern Tasmania. During the course of many floods, the trunk was damaged by floating debris and, eventually, several centuries ago, split down the centre, so only the landward half survived and continued to grow. More recently, the tree was undermined in yet another flood and washed downstream to where it came ashore and was recovered.

'The bird's eye markings in the timber represent a cluster of tiny shoots growing from the trunks where their growth has been stimulated, presumably by an infection. These shoots, not more than 3mm ($^1/_8$") in diameter, persist for centuries and become embedded as the trunk itself continues to grow in diameter.

'The wildly irregular log was first cut into blocks with a chainsaw, in such a way as to obtain the best yield of its usable timber. Part of the log was long dead and part recently alive, but all was saturated with water from its immersion in the river.'

First Adrian rough-turned this particular block, in common with all others, immediately. It was cut into a rough disc with the chainsaw and the surface which was to be the top of the bowl was screwed onto a faceplate, using the ring of screw holes closest to the centre of the faceplate. This was to enable the recovery of the centre of the block in one piece for the turning of a second bowl.

As the bowl block was out of balance, Adrian used a low lathe speed and the face of the block was turned with a 16mm ($^5/_8$") deep fluted gouge. A 10mm ($^3/_8$") detail gouge was then used to shape a spigot which would later become the foot of the bowl. This spigot was parallel sided and larger in diameter than the intended size of the foot, to allow for shrinkage during drying.

The deep fluted gouge was then used to shape the outside of the bowl. At this stage, the shape of the block was as shown in the diagram.

The faceplate was removed and the blank was reversed, being mounted in a four-jaw, self-centring chuck. As the block was now better balanced, it was possible for Adrian to raise the lathe speed. The face was trued with the deep fluted gouge and the centre was removed in one piece with a McNaughton centre saving tool. Some further shaping of the inside of the bowl was done with the 16mm (^{5}/$_8$'') deep fluted gouge.

Then Adrian waxed the bowl blank in order to slow the drying process and reduce the chance of it splitting. It was put aside for about ten months and was then assessed as dry enough to finish. This assessment Adrian did simply by feel: dry timber does not feel as cold to the touch as green timber.

In the re-turning process, the spigot on the bowl base was again gripped in the four-jaw, self-centring chuck; a detail gouge was then used to cut a square step into the inside of the bowl, as shown in the diagram.

The bowl was reversed and the chuck jaws were expanded into this step. The base was again trued and a detail gouge used to cut a recess of 52mm (2'') diameter in the centre of the foot. This was about 3mm (^{1}/$_8$'') deep and was undercut to match the shape of the jaws of the chuck which was to be used to support the bowl in the next stage.

The outside of the foot was then shaped with a detail gouge and a deep fluted gouge was used to shape the outside of the bowl as far as the point at which it turns in. Power sanding, with 50mm (2'') diameter discs, was used to smooth the outside, as well as some hand sanding in the undercut of the mounting recess. Sanding was done with grits between 100 and 400.

Adrian then applied a first coat of oil, rubbed in with fine steel wool.

The bowl was reversed for the last time and was mounted on a four-jaw, self-centring scroll chuck, with its dovetail jaws expanded into the recess in the base. As this was only 3mm (^{1}/$_8$'') deep, all further turning had to be done gently. The diameter of the recess matched the diameter at which the chuck jaws formed a true circle, so there was contact all round.

A 12mm (^{1}/$_2$'') deep fluted gouge was used to shape the upper part of the outside of the bowl and then to produce the undercut of the bowl rim. This was done before reducing the thickness of the body of the bowl, so there would be as little flexing as possible while working on the rim. The 16mm (^{5}/$_8$'') deep fluted gouge was then used to turn the lower part of the inside of the bowl, using a cutting action rather than a scraping one, and with the bevel of the tool rubbing at all times.

Power sanding was again used and an initial coat of oil rubbed in. After 24 hours, a second coat of oil was applied, left for some hours to dry, and then rubbed vigorously with a cloth. On this occasion, the oil used was Organoil Interior Oil.

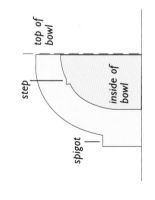

top of bowl

spigot

faceplate

top of bowl

step

inside of bowl

spigot

The Deepings Dolls

One of Adrian Hunt's most successful outputs, there are now more than 100 shapes for the Deepings Dolls. They are all turned out of white Tasmanian sassafras (*Atherosperma moschatum*) because of its even colour and freedom from knots. It also takes inks well and does not discolour with age.

The Deepings Dolls are painted by a team of painters, but the Noah set, shown here, is painted by Jilli Roberts. Jilli works under a lamp and first prepares the wood surface, and then works out the overall design and colour balance, together with placement of hands, arms and objects. Then she begins the fine linework with a dip-in mapping pen.

All the work is done with inks rather

Deepings Dolls – The Noahs 12cm (5") high approximately

than paint, although perhaps a small amount of gouache is mixed in to create a more opaque effect. All the work must be done quickly and confidently as the hot lamp dries the ink rapidly.

Colour is applied with tiny brushes and washes are mixed as required. Fabric textures are created by using the inks in various ways to create illusions of rough homespun, for example, and drapery linework is an important way to create the effect of fabric.

The Noah set includes as many animals as possible and Jilli loves to paint the miniature creatures, down to the last whiskers. Each set of Noahs is different from the one before, with the introduction of new animals or animal combinations on each piece.

After all this is completed, Jilli adds the faces to the dolls. This is the moment when the persona must come alive and the pen is allowed to guide the moment. Of course, Noah must have dignity, but sometimes a quirky eyebrow may suggest he has just sighted a pair of hippos or lions in the queue. Mrs Noah must be serene, but occasionally she has a touch of amusement in her eye. And Noah's sons show a range of emotions, from resignation to bemused surprise and joy.

Finally, the pieces are sealed to enhance the colour and preserve their durability.

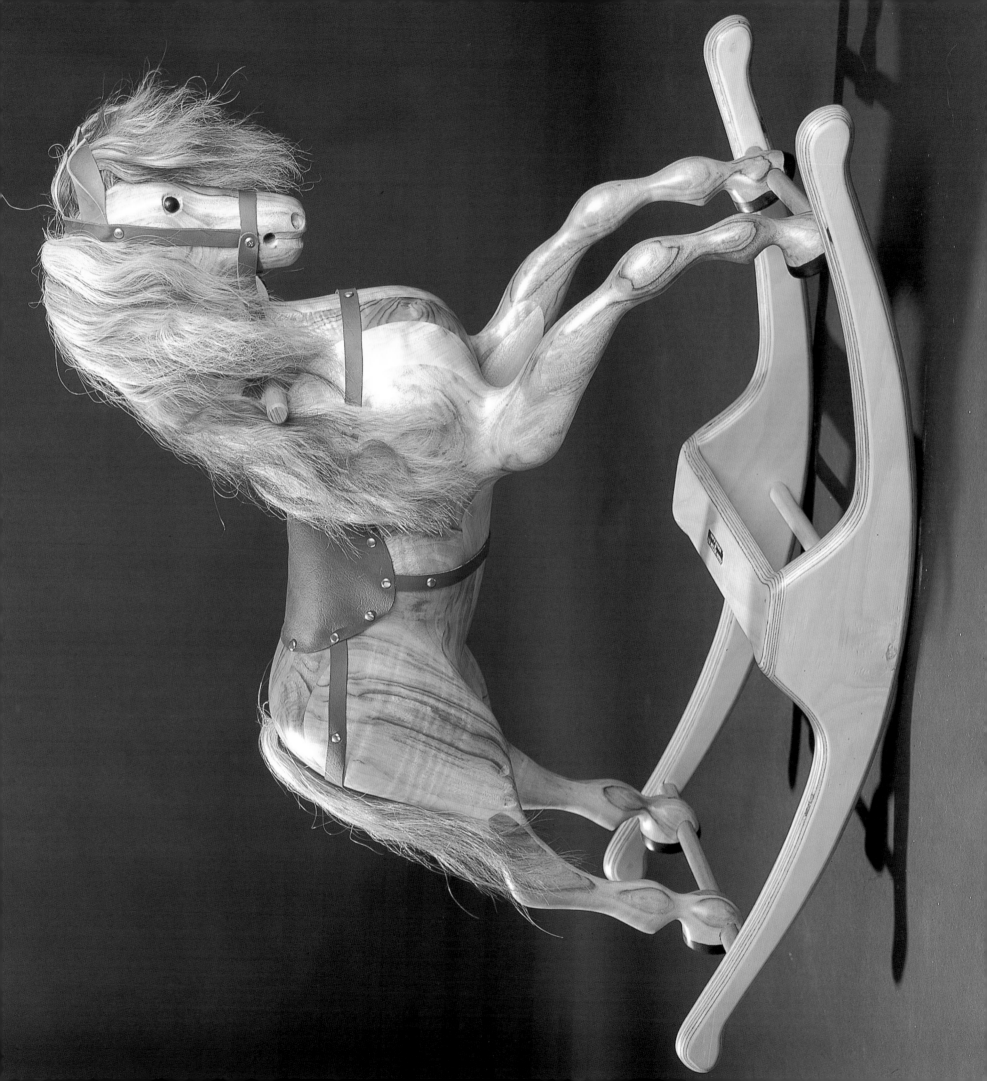

Don Metcalfe

Don Metcalfe is a timber sculptor with no formal training but whose interest goes back to working on wood carvings as a child. His grandfather was a pattern maker who made wooden originals which were used to make castings for production moulds. He made anything from wood, from a car's internal combustion engine to the propeller of the Queen Mary. Don, however, has turned these family skills to the production of functional and commercial artwork. His work ranges from classical style tables, vanities and kitchens to contemporary free-flowing tables and chairs. For the past seven years he has built a small business specialising in a unique breed of Australian rocking horses.

Don's approach to his craft work is a holistic one, firmly founded on the ideal of sustainability. On their property, he and his partner have established a seedling nursery, 3 hectares (6½ acres) of cabinet timber and eucalypt woodlot and a large solar wood drying kiln. Don's rocking horses and furniture are typically made from Australian cabinet timbers derived from salvage or plantation logs of hoop pine, silky oak, rosewood or cedar, or weed species such as camphor laurel. For every mature tree he harvests from his property, he aims to grow a hundred more. He plants the trees and mulches them with the sawdust and woodchips left over from the trees he has harvested so there is no waste.

Traditionally, rocking horses are a hollow box construction with the legs morticed onto the sides, but Don's rocking horses reflect his background as a sculptor. His horses are built up from layers of solid timber. He begins with a laminating process which involves joining layers or plates of pre-cut timber together achieving an approximation of the desired shape and thickness. This offers great freedom in the shaping process which follows but also offers logistical challenges. First, the timber used must be well dried, ideally to less than 13 per cent moisture content – this means kiln drying – and the timber must glue and machine well. Grain direction is also taken into account to maximise strength and minimise shrinkage.

Once the solid blank is created Don rough sculpts it using a carving wheel on a grinder and a rotary chisel which works in a similar way to a chainsaw. He follows this by finer sculpting using a grinder disc and orbital sanding. The result is a very realistic looking horse.

The horse is dressed with leather saddlery and cow hair is used to provide a lively mane and tail in a variety of tones. Finally, the horses are mounted on either rockers or swing stands. Because of their unique construction the horses are strong enough to take the weight of an adult as well as generations of enthusiastic children.

Rocking horse camphor laurel, 90cm high x 45cm wide x 120cm long (36" x 18" x 48")

Don Metcalfe

Wombat – Tasmanian blackwood, ebony, Huon pine 40cm x 60cm (16" x 24"). Platypus – Brazilian teak, American walnut, ebony, Brazilian walnut 35cm x 40cm (14" x 16")

Emily Hurt

Australiana, that form of design which promotes Australian images, seems to have lost favour over the years, but these wooden carvings by Emily Hurt are perennially popular. Never sentimental, Emily's animals and birds are often larger than life and are produced with great zest and humour using a wide range of woods.

Arriving from Boston about 35 years ago, living in a small flat and with few friends, Emily began 'whittling' away at a packing case when her husband went to work. Completely self-taught, she started carving wood, using her husbands tools, then gradually experimented with other more advanced tools and created these original ideas.

Emily draws a puzzle picture and cuts out the pieces. She then draws these pieces on her chosen woods and cuts them out. Each piece is glued onto a backing and shaped separately, then they are unglued and put together again on backing board cut out to the final shape. They take many hours of work – the platypus only about 10, but the wombat about 50 hours, while the kookaburra takes much more.

Kookaburra
Huon pine, ebony, American walnut, sassafras, silky oak, she oak, Tasmanian fiddleback blackwood, red box
65cm x 60cm (26" x 24")

Emily Hurt

Wave II handcarved Australian red cedar 15cm x 50cm x 33cm (6" x 20" x 13")

Robert Howard

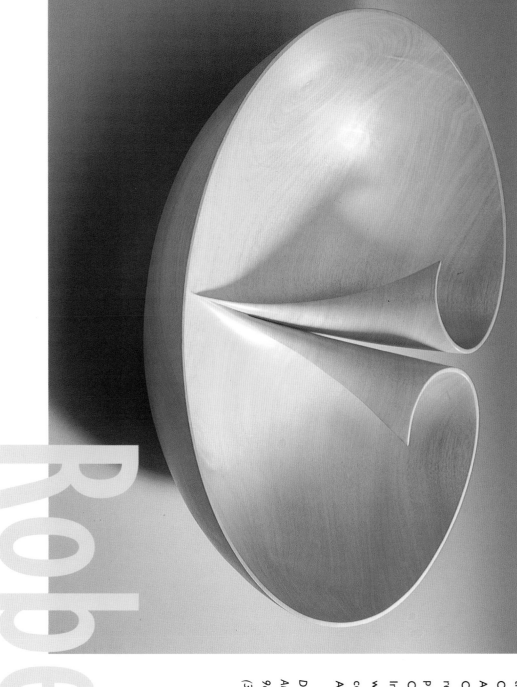

Meticulous hand work is Robert Howard's trademark. His beautifully organic, smooth vessels, which look more like sculptural pieces than wooden bowls, are painstakingly handcarved. This is a slow, incremental process which requires hard physical labour and intense concentration. The results are seemingly simple forms which are pure and elegant and which glow with the warmth of the wood.

Trained as a mechanical engineer, then later a cabinetmaker, now Robert's work includes sculptural chairs, although the bowls are his passion and they are coveted by collectors from the United States of America, Korea, Japan, France and Australia. Recent showing of his work at the prestigious Sculpture, Objects and Functional Art Show (SOFA) in Chicago, USA, has resulted in his work being purchased for the Bohlen Collection of the Detroit Institute of Art, and the well known wood collection of Ronald and Anita Wornich.

Dual drape – handcarved Australian white beech
9cm x 33cm x 28cm
(3¹/₂" x 13" x 11")

Robert

Howard

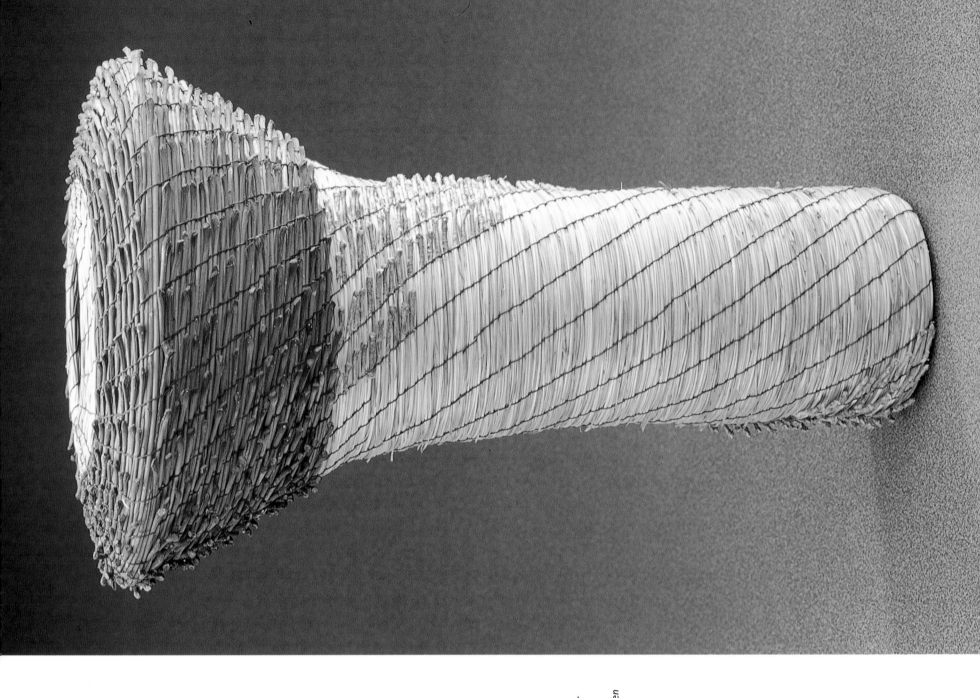

Blue & black, light & darker
Pine needle and jacaranda
stitched with cotton and linen
42.5cm (16³/4") high

Virginia Kaiser

S imple, elegant shapes, shaded in subtle hues, are the hallmark of Virginia Kaiser's basketry works. She creates small sculptural pieces, predominantly vessels, and her emphasis is on form, colour contrasts and textures, using plant fibres and basketry techniques. Her current work has been inspired by the forms of the native American baskets she saw during an Australia Council sponsored residency in the United States, although the colours are very much Australian – desert, sunset and earth.

Virginia has also combined some of her basketry techniques with the carved wood of Robert Howard to create stunning vessels which display the beauty and compatibility of natural materials. Intensely interested in environmental issues, these, and all her works, speak clearly of her respect for the environment and the value she places on natural timbers, grasses and other flora.

Virginia keeps a simplicity and fluidity in her shapes and harmonises the materials and techniques to compliment the form.

Virginia Kaiser

Fibre Basketry

This is a craft which is thought to date from almost the time of the first humans. It is an ancient craft which is still practised today with little more than hands and the fibres and plants grown and gathered for that purpose. More and more natural materials are being discovered by the basket makers of Australia and new techniques are being developed along the way. Some man made fibres are also being incorporated, but in only a minimal way as the natural colours of the plant materials, the fawns, browns, yellows, dark purples, greys and creams offer such subtle and beautifully muted shades.

Many native plants fibres are suitable for basketry, including clematis, flax-lily, rolling spinifex, kangaroo paw, cabbage palm, cumbungi, tussock sedge, she-oak, silver wattle and much more. Other suitable introduced plants include, among many more, banana, couch grass, gladiolus, iris, jacaranda, jasmine, date palm, passion flower, sweet corn, watsonia, wireweed, wisteria. In most cases the plant material is dried throroughly and then, before use, it is dampened again to make it pliable.

Many of the women basket makers featured in these pages have studied the methods of the Australian Aborigines and have mastered some of their techniques and incorporated them into their own work. They have certainly often been inspired by the shapes and practical forms of their vessels and carrying baskets. Others have been influenced by the methods and the forms of the Native North Americans. But all would acknowledge that this is a craft where the skills have been handed down for thousands of years and which must be preserved and respected.

Date palm fruit fronds – raw material for Hugh (opposite)

Nancy Duggan

W ith her work represented in major art and craft collections across Australia, Nancy Duggan is one of the most highly respected of basket makers. A regular teacher, she has inspired many others to take up this craft. On this page we show two of her beautiful baskets, both stitched in spiral stitch. *Jacaranda XXXIX* is worked in jacaranda with *Xanthorroea* resin. *Hugh* is made from date palm fruit fronds with boar tusks.

Left: Jacaranda
25cm (10") diameter

Far left: Hugh
37cm (14 ¹/₂") high

Nancy

Duggan

Old Vines and Woven Fibres

Pat Dale

Like the work of many basket makers today, Pat Dale's basket pieces have evolved, moving away from highly constructed forms to more creative expressions. Working with natural fibre since about 1963, she was inspired by the work of American Douglass Fuchs and attended his workshop in 1982. She has since travelled to conferences and workshops in the United States, Fiji and New Zealand, learning traditional techniques and experimenting with new ones. Since 1987 she has led cultural tours to Indonesia and coordinated exhibitions of baskets there.

Pat's work is innovative and she often uses new or unusual techniques. She feels no need to conform to traditional basketry techniques, preferring instead to use what suits to control the material at hand in order to achieve her contemporary shapes.

A well known teacher and author of a recent book on basketry, Pat has been involved in community crafts for more than 30 years. Now she is dedicated to her craft of basketry. 'I have a strong physical involvement with the work, starting from collecting materials, to the development of the idea, to the planning of the concept – and then wrestling with the construction.' She enjoys working with her materials, particularly the vines. 'I want to feel the history and the life of old vines, warts and all.'

In *Tribal bowl of the Warra-Burra*, Pat has used the Australian native vine Kennedia, for the framework. Australian *Cordyline stricta* and iris leaves make up the woven material and they promote the dark and light colours. The butt end of *Cordyline stricta* has provided the texture on the rim.

The wisteria vine used in *Offering basket* (see introduction) had been collected and twisted into shape months before Pat employed it in her work. Wisteria vine was used for the frame and iris leaves for the weaving material.

Tribal bowl of the Warra-Burra
20cm high x 31cm wide x 20 cm
deep (8" x 12¼" x 8")

Pat Dale

Reconciliation

Judy Grey-Gardner

This piece was created by Judy Grey-Gardner for the Fibre Basket Weavers of South Australia's reconciliation exhibition entitled 'Links'. The inspiration came from the Sea of Hands for Reconciliation, which toured the country.

The hand in the sculpure is made using the Ngarrindjeri method of basketry and uses their traditional rushes, *Cyperus gymnocaulus*. The work is mounted, with roots to the earth, on a piece of driftwood.

Judy harvested rushes, dried them (to avoid shrinkage) then dampened them again so that they were pliable and ready to use. She made a core with about seven or eight rushes, then, using another single strand, worked blanket stitches around them. In the second row each stitch was made into the first row of stitching.

The Finger Puppets were made with a core of the chosen fibre (dried, then dampened) and stitched using basketweaver's buttonhole stitch (linen thread was used here). In the second row the stitch was made into the core material beside the stitch in the first row. The materials used were (from thumb): winter flowering iris; (*Unguicalaris*); flag iris (*Germanica*); *Aristea ensifolia*; sweet corn husks (*Zea mays*); Watsonia

Friends
36cm x 29cm (14" x 11 1/2")

New Zealand Flax and Wool

Helen Richardson

n 1975 Helen Richardson undertook an Art and Craft Certificate Course where basketry was her final elective. Many of the basketry students continued to meet afterwards on a regular basis and as a result the Fibre Basket Weavers of South Australia was formed in 1981. While there are now many groups and fibre artists throughout Australia this has possibly been the most influential organisation, continuing to meet regularly and with many interstate members. Helen was the main organiser, researcher, writer and editor of the book *Fibre Basketry Homegrown and Handmade*, published in 1989, which recorded the group's joint experience and knowledge, and which contains not only examples of work, but full and detailed instructions on different basketry methods. While much basketry today is contemporary and experimental, this information is still of vital importance in providing the bases for all other techniques.

Helen has never been a prolific basket maker and now combines basketry with her other loves of spinning, weaving, natural dyeing and felt making.

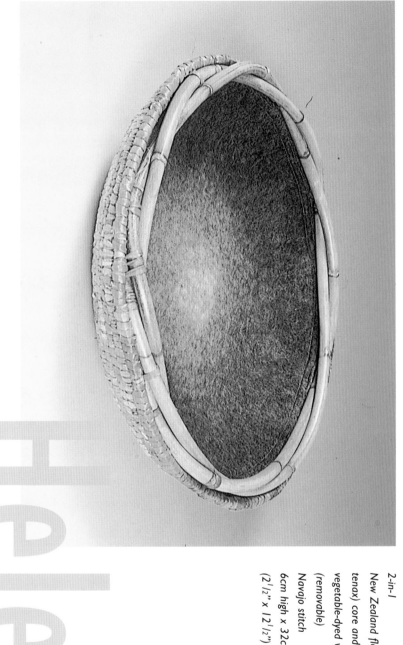

2-in-1
New Zealand flax (Phormium tenax) core and wrapping, vegetable-dyed woollen felt lining (removable)
Navajo stitch
6cm high x 32cm diameter (2$^1/_2$" x 12$^1/_2$")

Helen Richardson

11cm high x 46cm long x 39cm wide (4¹/₄” x 18” x 15¹/₄”)
New Zealand flax, ginger nut stems, canna leaves, Solomon seal
stems, walnut dyed seagrass, Watsonia, chasmanthe

Sally King

Knowing already how to make baskets in cane, Sally King saw American Douglas Fuchs' exhibition 'Floating Forests' in the early 80s and was inspired to begin making baskets from soft natural fibres. Many basket makers were similarly inspired by this exhibition and a conference was held in Melbourne in 1986 where Sally was finally able to find a teacher. She has been making baskets ever since, although recently she has scaled down her production to study glass making.

The first of Sally's baskets shown here was made from red hot poker (*Kniphofia* spp.). She explains her choice. 'This plant is easily grown in the garden and is excellent for basket making in that it can be gathered at any time, tied in bundles and hung to dry in a shaded dry area. Before weaving I place as many bundles as required on the grass, give them a quick squirt with the hose and wrap them firmly in an old dry sheet and leave them, preferably for two nights, to mellow.'

In this basket the leaves were twined over strands of New Zealand flax and the 'boucle' string was made for the central part of the bowl. The colour in the leaves became more prominent in the border area where a simple wrapping technique was used.

In the second basket, colours, textures and variations of weaving techniques were used. This basket was woven over a frame made from palambang. Most of the colours are natural but the seagrass was dyed using black walnut hulls resulting in two different shades. DAS was mixed with Aquadhere glue and applied afterwards when Sally painted it on and blended it with the other materials. Techniques used in this basket were twining, single strand weaving and wrapping.

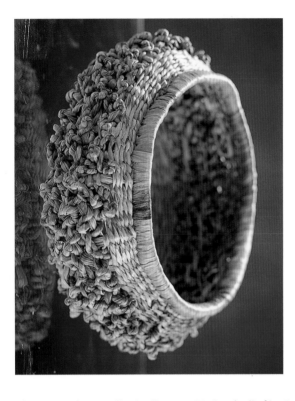

13cm high x 33cm diameter (5" x 13")
red hot poker leaves, New Zealand flax

Sally King

Geomorphic form

coilbuilt and carved

patinated copper matt glazes

39cm x 37cm (15 $^1/_2$" x 14 $^1/_2$")

Jeff Mincham

These large, masculine forms, with subtle, tranquil, landscape surfaces, are the result of rigorous and physical labour from this potter who has been working for more than 20 years. Jeff Mincham's current work grew out of the Raku he used to practise, which is where a flame leaves a spontaneous and unpredictable coloured impression on the clay surfaces.

He achieves these works through a process which involves several firings. After coiling, carving, and initial glazing, they are rapid fired at 1100°C (2012°F) (subsequent firings are at lower temperatures) so naturally the clay body has to be solid enough to tolerate this. He has a very large kiln so he can make larger works and he applies his colour surfaces during the cooling stages. He takes the pieces out of the kiln at 400°C (752°F) which he calls 'burning glove' stage. The smaller pieces he can lift out using tongs when they are very hot, but for the big works he wears a leather coat, an apron, a face shield and two pairs of leather gloves. The gloves can catch fire, hence his description.

He then uses sprays and brushes to apply the colours and a blowtorch to burn them in. As he says, 'It would be nice to have someone else to hold the blowtorch but it is all a bit dangerous, so

Geomorphic vessel
coilbuilt and carved
patinated copper matt glazes
48cm x 32cm x 21cm (19" x 12 1/2" x 8 1/4")

it is better done alone.' This secondary glazing must be done in 10 minutes or the piece begins to cool and crack. It is then returned to the kiln for cooling. The loss rate can be particularly high.

The glazes have been formulated to be especially reactive to these treatments and have very high metal contents (usually copper) but also have matt, slightly absorbent, surfaces, that produce 'watercolour like' effects which, being semi accidental, echo the spontaneity of the Raku process.

Jeff has chosen to refer to the type of surface effect as 'Patination' as it roughly equates with the patination processes used on metals, particularly bronze, and he makes extensive use of a variety of metal chlorides, nitrates and poly sulphides to produce a kind of sped up weathering process, on surfaces which are especially receptive to such treatment. His title of 'geomorphic' for some of his works seems apt as they have a quality similar to the layers of the earth's substrata.

Headland
ceramic wall panel
patinated ceramic glazes
27cm x 64cm x 4cm
(10$^{1}/_{2}$" x 25$^{1}/_{2}$" x 1$^{3}/_{4}$")

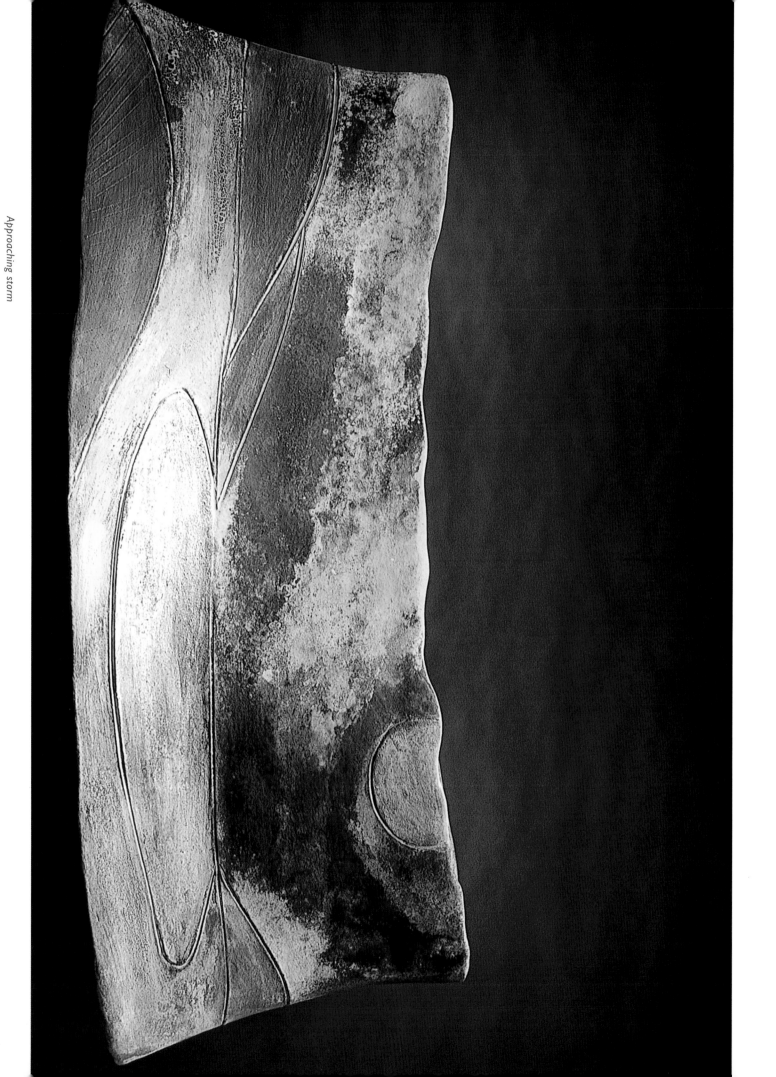

Approaching storm
coilbuilt elliptical vessel patinated copper matt glazes
24cm x 65cm x 19cm (9½" x 26" x 7½")

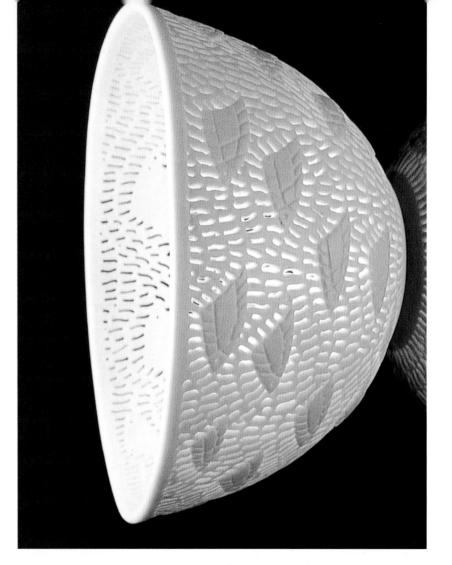

Pierced and carved fish bowl porcelain (above)
6.5cm high x 12cm wide (2^1/$_2$" x 4^3/$_4$")

Grey Madonna, bone china, draped
43.5cm high x 5cm at base and 11cm at top (17" x 2" x 4 ^{1}/$_4$")

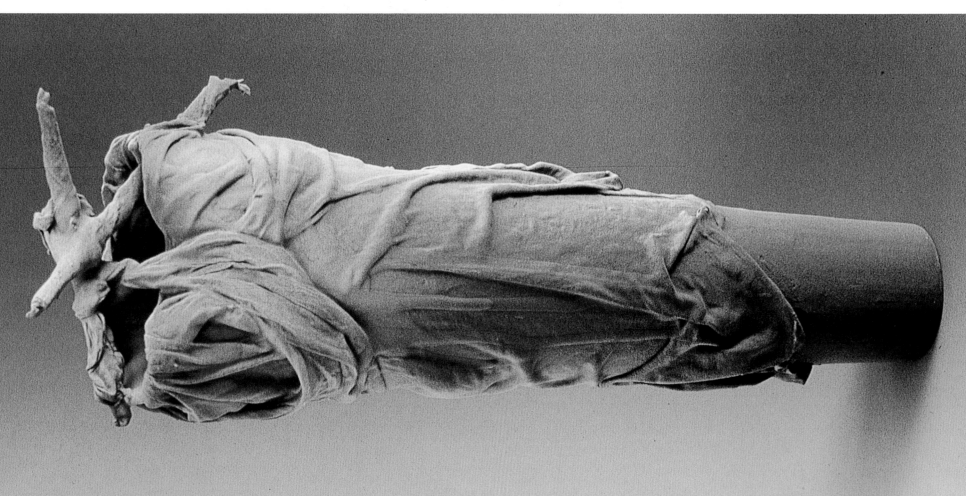

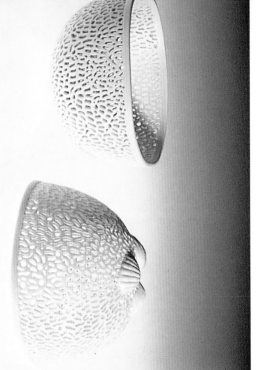

Porcelain and Bone China

Sandra Black

W orking with porcelain since the late 1970s, Sandra Black was drawn by its qualities of translucence, whiteness and fine surface. She is best known for her pierced works and carved pieces. The lace-like effect of the pierced works exploits the strength and light transmitting qualities of the porcelain, creating intricate patterns of light and shadow and, in carved works, she makes complex Escher-like patterns as shown in her *Daintree* series. These works were inspired by the rainforests of North Queensland as well as the carved incense burners found on a trip to Japan.

Sandra's pierced and carved works are about the exploration of light and shadow, pattern making and refinement of form and image. Technically, she finds them engaging and challenging, pushing the boundaries of her skills. Despite their apparent complexity, they are also meditative for her during the carving process. The piercing and cleaning processes however require intense concentration.

Sandra's draped forms, for which she is also renowned, were made from late 1986 – 1992. They were an attempt to resolve grief and loss. The result was a body of work of figurative based pieces and also well like vessels which came from the figurative works and drew on the classical period with the use of draping as well as images from contemporary film. Japanese art and architectural references. In the figurative pieces, such as *Grey Madonna* the form is wrapped and bound. There are no arms or legs. Everything is bound, encased and immobile, locked into grief. But it is still also a gentle and contemplative piece.

Since 1988 the work has shifted and changed, as issues and life resolved themselves. Sandra drew less on her grief but more on a sense of renewal and completion. Later work in this series tended to draw inspiration from fantasy and social issues.

Pierced shell footed porcelain vessels
6.5cm high x 9.5cm wide (2$^{1}/_{2}$" x 3$^{3}/_{4}$")

Sandra Black

Carving Porcelain

Sandra carves into leather-hard porcelain, using a minimum of tools:

Requirements

No 11 Swann Morton surgical blade in a cane holder

soft brush	sponge
water spray	fine steel wool grade 00 – 000

Prior to carving Sandra throws about 24 pots. These are turned and stored in an old freezer to keep damp. Pots need to be of correct thickness though this comes with practice. Too thick and the porcelain looses its delicacy, too thin and it will crack during carving or slump in the firing. About 2mm ($1/16''$) is a good thickness. Bowls should be fractionally thicker near the bottom to prevent slumping.

Sandra draws the design onto the form with the tip of the carving blade. She builds up the design piece by piece rather than drawing the complete pattern. The pattern is cut in about 1mm ($1/32''$) and then the blade is used on its side to cut away excess clay and leave a relief pattern. The tip of the blade is then used to draw a line around each area of relief to sharpen the design. A soft brush is used to remove small particles of clay without damaging the design. A damp sponge is used to soften the sharp edges and smooth the surface.

Carving can be elaborate, but only experience can tell how far to go. Sandra believes it is best to carve out lots of small areas supported by small columns of clay rather than a large one. Large carved areas can collapse without support or split the pot in half. Carving on one side of a bowl can cause the form to deform or oval in the firing. This can be deliberately done to alter shapes in a subtle way. When dry, the form can be gently rubbed with steel wool to soften and clean up the carving and throwing lines. All the dust and steelwool fibres must be removed. Compressed air can be used to blow off the dust in a spray booth or it can be done outside where dust won't be inhaled.

After a low bisque of 850°C – 900°C (1562°F – 1652°F) the carved works are soaked in water then gently re-sanded with wet and dry sandpaper of grade 400 – 600. They are rinsed off well to get rid of silicon carbide grit. Generally, most of the work is left unglazed and repolished after the high temperature firing at cone 10.

A good reliable clear glaze for porcelain is as follows. It has a low thermal expansion and can fire over a range of 1220°C (2230°F) to 1280°C (2335°F). Ball milling will improve its quality.

Nepheline syenite	29.3	Whiting	9.7
Barium carbonate	6.4	Zinc oxide	7.9
Talc	3.9	China clay	10.1
Ball clay	5.0	Silica	27.7

Care must be taken in application of this glaze not to apply it too thickly and thus obscure the design. Correctly applied it won't run and any unevenness will smooth out. This glaze does not work over some of the coloured stains and will alter their appearance. This is due to the zinc oxide content in the glaze.

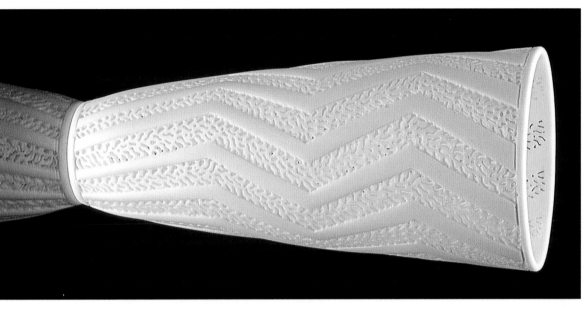

Zig Zag Vessel, pierced and carved porcelain.
19cm (7¹/₂") high x 8.5cm (3¹/₂") at top

Bone china is somewhat more difficult to glaze. It is better to high fire to semi translucency and then use a low fire brush on glaze to cover the carving, or leave it unglazed and highly polished.

Piercing

Piercing works very well in slip cast porcelain or bone china and thrown porcelain. A small electric drill and dental bits are used to do the piercing at the leather hard stage. Care must be taken if the cast is damp, as sections of the wall will tend to collapse with the thixotropic nature of casting bodies. The vibration of the drill causes this. Alternatively, if the clay is too dry it will crack and pit. Sandra uses a Dremmel drill and has a collection of fine drill bits from Dremmel and dentist supplies.

Cleaning up is carried out at the dry stage when the surface is sanded smooth. This is best done with fine steel wool. Cleaning out of dust is done by using a compressor to blow dust out of the holes. A dust mask is worn for this process. Further polishing is done after the bisque. The piece is soaked in water to eliminate dust and polished with wet and dry paper grades 300 and 600.

Firing is undertaken at the appropriate temperatures for the various casting or thrown bodies. The design of these pieces must be carefully considered. The thinness of the walls makes them prone to collapse. Some shapes may need to be fired on their rims to avoid this. Piercing on one section of a form can also cause the work to oval in the firing so you must experiment with the form to enhance this or stop it. The pieces are also repolished after the glaze firing.

Draped work

Soft cotton fabrics and other absorbent materials can be draped over sculptural cast forms. A soft cotton mull which is first washed and dried is suitable. The basic form is prepared for draping by slip casting the form and bringing it to a dry leather-hard stage. The fabric is then dipped into the casting slip and quickly arranged around the form. Once the fabric is in place the work is placed in front of a fan to dry as quickly as possible before it collapses with the extra moisture. The form is turned regularly so it doesn't warp. Once the form has firmed up Sandra strengthens the surfaces by injecting extra slip in behind the folds. She then airbrushes some extra slip over the top of the fabric and applies any colours to the work by brushing or air brushing while leather- hard. The works are then once fired, as they are too fragile to handle in the bisque stage. If surfaces need touching up again the work can be heated, re-sprayed and re-fired.

Large Southern Ice open porcelain bowl
Forest Floor
deep etched 25.5cm high x 28cm diameter (10" x 11")

Large oval porcelain bowl
Kyoto Flower
deep etched 35cm high x 48cm diameter (13³/₄" x 19")

Les Blakebrough

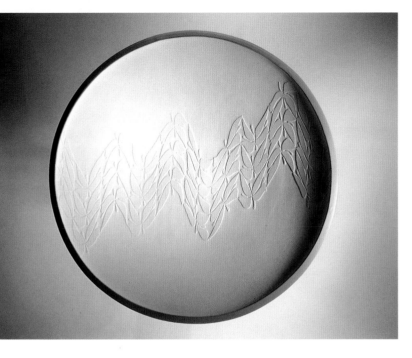

The elegant, fine and delicate forms created by Les Blakebrough show clearly his consummate skill, achieved through years of work in this medium – since 1957 – as well as a thorough understanding of materials and processes.

His classic, almost pristine handmade work seems to belie his interest in, and study of, the 'industrial' methods of producing pottery – manufacturing, on a smaller scale, if you like. He trained in Australia and Japan, and was for many years living the Arcadian dream of a country potter, but his years in Kyoto, Japan, and his later study tour of the major porcelain factories in Scandinavia and the United Kingdom, revealed to him that an individual's 'designs' could be 'manufactured' by others. Whilst away he found the luxury of designing at a drawing desk and computer, working out carefully all the details, unlike the imprecise method of designing as a piece is thrown on a wheel and working out the design through that process. He marvelled at the ability of the workers, more highly skilled and practised at their individual tasks than any one person could be while attempting to be self sufficient.

Now, as well as teaching, Les is involved in research projects at the University of Tasmania in Hobart, to discover ways of utilising industrial processes and applying them to craft based ceramics. Yet, while trying to advance the cause of craft based workshops which could produce consistently high quality work, he says, 'The enjoyment of materials and process remains a strong and abiding aspect of what I do, I am never likely to abandon that, or making individual work by hand'.

His recent work utilises a very white and translucent form of porcelain he has called Southern Ice. This relates to the particular part of the world which has inspired and influenced him – Tasmania and the Great Southern Ocean, where he lives, works and plays. Antarctica is not far away and its terrible beauty is always a fascination. Les has created on the unglazed surfaces of this porcelain some unusual effects using water soluble metallic salts which develop a 'halo' effect. He has also deep etched the surfaces of those shown here, leaving a beautiful white on white pattern. The patterns themselves reflect his attention to the detail of his surroundings, for example the patterns of light on leaves, or on water, also remembered patterns of flowers from his time in Kyoto.

Large porcelain bowl
Kyoto Flower - mellowed by time and memory
deep etched 45cm diameter (17³/₄")

Les
Blakebrough

Desert Secrets – Eastern Goldfields Series III
porcelain with lustre
26cm (11") high

Rite of Passage – Ubirr– North Series I 65.5cm (26") high

Untitled – North Series II
porcelain with gold lustre,
10 carat
37cm (14¹/₂") high

Pippin Drysdale

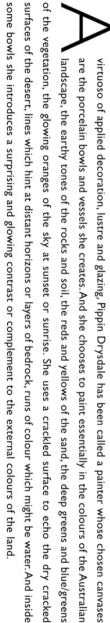

Desert Illuminations –
North Series II
c. 34cm (13 ¹/₂") high
porcelain with platinum lustre

A virtuoso of applied decoration, lustre and glazing, Pippin Drysdale has been called a painter whose chosen canvases are the porcelain bowls and vessels she creates. And she chooses to paint essentially in the colours of the Australian landscape, the glowing oranges of the sky at sunset or sunrise. She uses a crackled surface to echo the dry cracked surfaces of the desert, lines which hint at distant horizons or layers of bedrock, runs of colour which might be water. And inside some bowls she introduces a surprising and glowing contrast or complement to the external colours of the land.

Pippin's relationship with the landscape is profound and personal and she is driven by a need to capture its essential beauty through a simplicity of form and a depth of colour. These porcelain vessels record her journeys through Australia's unique and varied environments.

After years of study both within Australia and overseas, and with hundreds, if not thousands, of pieces behind her, Pippin shows great command of her work although she is always experimenting and researching, particularly decorative glazes and her distinctive layered three dimensional surfaces.

Pippin makes and prepares her own glazes, developing the palette she will use on a series. She then trials these colours on shards to test that they fuse at the same temperature and will be true to their colour under several layers of glaze. This might take several weeks before she can begin a series.

The porcelain vessels are hand thrown and then turned inside and out at the leather-hard stage. Once they are dry they are fired and then follows the lengthy decorating process.

The pot is sandpapered, sponged lightly back and allowed to dry overnight. The next day the base application is sprayed on and allowed to dry overnight. Then the piece is rubbed back to remove the excess glaze and the dust from this process is removed carefully.

Then each piece is handpainted using a diluted version of the base glaze to create a smooth surface on which to work the decorative elements.

After drying again overnight, special wax and latex resists are applied either over or under colours, depending on the effects Pippin wishes to achieve. Only after firing can she be absolutely sure the results are exactly as she wishes and although she discards numerous examples of her work, every firing teaches her something more about her glazes and lustres.

Pippin
Drysdale

Handbuilt Ceramics

Hiroe Swen

A lthough recently retired, Hiroe Swen continues her commitment to teaching ceramics. Appointed a Visiting Fellow to the Australian National University Institute of the Arts, Canberra, after 19 years of lecturing there, she shows little sign of slowing down. Now in her mid-60s, she still produces a significant body of handbuilt ceramics, which are exhibited internationally and nationally, especially at her own Pastoral Gallery.

Before coming to Australia in 1968, Hiroe trained in Kyoto, first as a painter and textile designer, later as a ceramist. She became the first woman to be accepted as an apprentice to the master potter H. Hayashi. During her five year ceramics training she exhibited regularly, culminating in entries in the prestigious Japanese National Art Society (Nitten) exhibitions, and she also founded the National Association of Women Potters in Japan.

Her energy, her output and her working schedule are prodigious, yet Hiroe produces ceramics which emanate a calm serenity. They are subtle and display the control of the master potter, sure of her technique. The works are deceptively simple, bordering on utilitarian, yet sculptured, with an understated decorative pattern resembling a private style of calligraphy. The glazes, with colours often blending into each other, add a sense of texture to Hiroe's pieces, their hues often reflecting the immediate landscape of the Southern Tablelands in which her studio is located and these pieces are produced.

Tree Shadows
25cm high x 20cm wide x 20cm deep (10" x 8" x 8")

Oceandwellers 2 (left)
20cm high x 14.5cm wide x 8cm deep (8" x 5 3/4" x 3 1/4")

Hiroe Swen

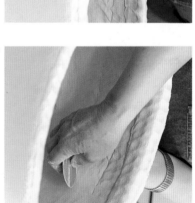

Coilbuilt

1. Hiroe paints slip around the edges of the prepared base.
2. She makes a large coil from the wedged clay, rolling it between her hands.
3. She lays the coil around the edges of the base and presses with her fingers inside and outside.
4. She continues to press and then pinches the top higher from the outside until it is about 5cm – 7cm (2" – 3").
5. A second coil is added, overlapping the first and they are squeezed together.
   It is then squeezed from the outside and pinched up until the sides are 12cm – 15cm (5" – 6"). (Another coil is added in the same way so the desired height is reached.)
6. After the clay dries to leatherhard, the bowl-form is cleaned up and smoothed with a blade.
   Finer and finer blades are used to achieve a smooth finish.
7. Because the lip of the bowl is thin, Hiroe adds an extra clay coil along the inside of the lip and presses it on with her fingers.
8. She cuts this coil back with a scalpel. She then uses her fingers to pinch and smooth the edges.
9. The bowl is then cleaned up on the inside with a circular blade.
10. Final clean up is done with a knife like blade and the finished work is ready for glazing and firing.

Oceanscape 3
25cm high x 28cm wide x 10cm deep (10" x 11" x 4")

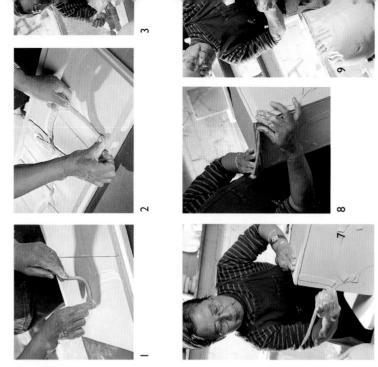

3

9

2

8

1

7

Completed forms ready for glazing and firing at 1260°C (2300°F).

Slabbuilt ceramics

Hiroe marks out her design on the prepared slabs of clay with a pencil. This design symbolises a tree, and is marked on each side of the ceramic. (See opening page.) She then adds slip (liquefied clay) to the area to be decorated.

1. She takes a small coil of clay and flattens it down on the decoration. She flattens the coil with her fingertips, leaving it thicker at one end. She smooths the flattened coil to different thicknesses with a blade.

2. Hiroe usually completes all four sides of the ceramic at the same time – adding slip, coil, pressing and smoothing.

3. Hiroe then builds the decorated slabs onto the base, gluing them with the slip. Here she adds clay along the join line.

4. She stands the side into position on the wet edges of the slab base.

5. The sides are joined to each other with a thin coil of extra clay.

6. When all the sides are complete Hiroe turns the work upside down to work on the base.

7. She tidies up the joins on the base and opens up a groove along the seam lines.

8. She paints on slip and pushes a thin coil of extra clay into the grooves .

9. She smooths this surface then Hiroe uses a scalpel to cut away the edges of the base, using a ruler to ensure they are cut straight. The work is turned over again and she fills the side joins with extra clay.

10. Hiroe makes a big coil of clay and lays it around the top edges, pressing it in with her fingers.

11. She then cuts roughly around the inside top edges with a scalpel.

12. After leaving to dry for about eight hours to leatherhard, Hiroe tidies up both inside and outside with blades.

13. The finished piece is ready for glazing and firing.

Cups and saucers
underglaze decoration
on-glaze enamel and gold lustre

Stephen Bowers

W ith a special skill for decoration, Stephen Bowers, while not unwilling to undertake all aspects of ceramic production, likes to work with others in order to complete all of the work required of him. He has worked with thrower Mark Heidenreich for many years, and he values this collaboration greatly.

Stephen's work depicts images of Australia and Australian wildlife, but it is a quirky representation, not simply a realistic copying of scenes, animals and birds. He is particularly amused by sulphur-crested cockatoos, which he refers to as 'some sort of white question mark', and they appear in many of his designs.

Stephen produces a highly popular range of tableware and other functional pieces but, as each piece is decorated by hand, orders must be restricted. He enjoys the fact that his pieces are used by their purchasers, and hopes that their hand made qualities might influence them in their daily lives. His interest in the functional nature of ceramics has led Stephen to be involved in setting up the current production line at the JamFactory Craft and Design Centre in Adelaide which incorporates a marbled effect in the desert colours of the region to the north.

While these functional pieces require an enormous amount of decoration and finishing, Stephen's one-off works of urns and platters, are a mammoth feat. Each of the one-off baluster vases, such as those shown here, might contain between 20 and 30 colours, require up to seven firings, with a high loss rate, and might spend up to four weeks in the kiln. He is rewarded with the recognition these pieces receive, the resultant commissions, and the awards and prizes he has won.

Cockatoos and foliage mutant chintzy urns
pair of baluster urns commissioned by Parliament House, Canberra
thrown on the wheel by Mark Heidenreich
decorated with underglaze brushwork and treatments with on-glaze gold lustre
95cm (38") high

Stephen Bowers

Grape bowl 35cm (14")

Lorraine Hansen

For more than 30 years Lorraine Hansen has devoted much of her life to china painting and is a life member of the Victorian Guild of China Painters. She is also a respected teacher and demonstrator both in Australia and overseas and has been awarded many prizes. Her many exhibitions are always popular. Now Lorraine is keenly interested in watercolour painting and has found time to study this art form too.

Lorraine's work, particularly her watercolours, are often of floral arrangements, reflecting her love of flowers and her earlier profession of floristry.

Grape Bowl

These grapes are painted in a different method, which builds up very strong and vibrant colours. This maintains the transparency of the grapes. This method is called 'Dry Dusting'.

Requirements

porcelain bowl approximately 36cm (14") in diameter

Porcelain On-Glaze paints mixed with Balsam of Copaiba: Black Green, Autumn Green, Chartreuse, Chestnut, Ochre, Mixing Yellow, Sèvres Pink, Ruby Red, Pansy Purple, Iris Brown, Baby Blue, Nansu Blue, Russian Green

Paint colours for 'dry dusting': Mixing Yellow, Pale Blue, Pansy Purple, Royal Purple (this is a Haida colour), Fay Goodi's Ruby Red, Sèvres Pink, Autumn Green

wipe out tool

brushes: Nuart short bristle brushes, ³/₄" (2cm), ¹/₂" (12mm), ¹/₄" (5mm), pointer, Josephine scroller No 1

First firing

Working quickly, block in the colour of the grapes and leaves. Form each grape individually in random patterns, as a three dimensional effect is wanted. Form one grape on top of a portion of another, and so on, preferably not in a straight line.

Come back with a wipe out tool and create a highlight on top of the grape and reflected light on the underside of the grape. Soften and blend.

Remember that light hits on one side of the grapes and bounces back. The grape is the same as any orb to paint, some in shadow and some in full light.

Establish any stems as a directional line by wiping out.

When the main design is complete, allow to dry for at least one hour, depending on the weather conditions.

Using a dry pallete of colour (dry powder paint not mixed with any medium) and a dry brush, paint again from light to dark over the subject matter.

Clean away all dry powder making sure there are no finger prints. Fire at 800°C (1470°F).

Second firing

Assess the painting and the depth. Is it as dark as it should be, are the grapes deep enough?

The background and the leaves now have to be brought up to an equal strength and still maintain the subtlety of the main leaves, while also maintaining the naturalistic look of the grape vine and the grapes hanging below the leaves and into the light.

Using warm colour, paint in the background and behind the leaves with Iris Brown. With Chestnut, Ochre and Mixing Yellow, paint these colours graduating down to the sunshine in the centre and around the bunches of grapes.

Paint in the Blues around the edge of the bowl to create the colour for the shadows.

Wipe back to the china for stems and branches of the vine and paint in the main branches. Fire at 800°C (1470°F).

Third firing

Strengthen the depth around the grapes using Ruby Red on the grapes hanging into the light, then Black Green behind the leaves, creating more background leaves.

Wash over the leaves with Autumn Green, Chartreuse and other warm autumn colours.

Paint in the stem and tendrils and wash depth into darkest areas. Fire at 800°C (1470°F).

Roses by the sea

(with thanks to Susan Irvine)

Requirements

Porcelain On-Glaze paints which are in powder form and are mixed with Balsam of Copaiba. Colours: Black Green, Autumn Green, Chartreuse, Chestnut, Ochre, Mixing Yellow, Dull Red (used very lightly to create a soft pink for the roses), Dusk Pink, Turquoise, Pansy Purple, Iris Brown Note: Colours are mixed on the brush as needed.

30cm (12") diameter white mount board of desired size, cut to fit round the porcelain

brushes: Nuart short bristle brushes, ³/₄"(2cm), ¹/₂"(12mm), ¹/₄" (5mm)

wipe out tool

pointer Josephine scroller No 1 watercolours to match porcelain paints

30cm (12") diameter porcelain, plus mount

white porcelain of desired shape, this one

Roses by the sea

Place and paint in the main design of roses, wiping back to the white of the china for the leading two roses in the centre of the design, adding a suggestion of green for the leaves and blue for the shadows

Wipe out the main set of leaves above the two main roses. Fire at 800°C (1470°F).

Sketch in design lines with a water based pen, adding leaves and buds. Plan the extension on to the mount board of the completed painting. Make any correction and plan to proceed to paint using Black Green for depth and Pansy Purple in the shadow areas, Ochre and Mixing Yellow for the light. Completely cover the porcelain with wet paint.

Paint in Blue as shadows on the roses and detail on the leaves. Wash a light colour over the background and wipe back some cutouts, creating a filtered shadow area. Add Iris Brown and Autumn Green to the stems and thorns. The shadows are now formed on the porcelain. Fire at 800°C (1470°F).

Assess the painting critically. Place a wash over the whole piece. Paint in any details, veins on leaves, and add some Ochre depth in the centre of the roses and deepen the calyx on the rosebuds.

Make any necessary corrections. Fire at 800°C (1470°F).

Lay the mount board over the porcelain, and, sketching very lightly with pencil, extend the design on to the mount, bringing the stems and the leaves out from the porcelain.

Anke Arkesteyn

Handmade tiles
13cm x 13cm x 5mm approximately
5^1/$_4$" x 5^1/$_4$" x ^{1}/$_5$"

T rained at the largest and most widely known ceramic establishment in Delft, Holland, Anke went on to study fine art followed by music which she taught in Holland and Germany. Migrating to Australia in 1983 she now plays the Celtic harp to relax after work as an artist producing handmade and specially designed tiles, plates, vases, urns and plaques.

Anke paints most of her works in the traditional blues of Delft, but her techniques can be used for many colours and designs.

Requirements – tile making

modelling clay firing at 1020°C – 1080°C (1870°F – 1970°F)

jig for moulding:

make a wooden base 30cm x 30cm (12" x 12"). From 10mm (2/5") thick strips of wood make a square with the internal measurements of 16.5cm x 16.5cm (6^1/$_2$" x 6^1/$_2$"). Nail or screw into the wood, ensuring these are below the surface

wet tile support:

from thin 4mm (^{1}/$_8$") plywood cut a square slightly less than 16.5cm x 16.5cm (6^1/$_2$" x 6^1/$_2$"), to fit loosely into the square on the moulding jig.

cellophane squares 16.5cm x 16.5cm (6^1/$_2$" x 6^1/$_2$") – 2 for each tile

trimmer – plywood square 14.5cm x 14.5cm (5^3/$_4$" x 5^3/$_4$")

cutting wire

straight edged scraper or steel ruler

knife or blade

thick cardboard 20cm x 20cm (8" x 8") approximately – 2 for each tile

Place the wet tile support inside the moulding jig. Lay one square of cellophane on top of the tile support.

1. Knead the clay and prepare a ball to overfill the moulding space. By pounding with your fist and pressing, fill all the corners and sides.

2. Draw the cutting wire towards you to remove any excess clay.

3. Pull a straight edged scraper or steel ruler towards you, held at an angle of 45°. Touch up any holes with damp clay and scrape again.

4. Free the edges of the wet tile from the mould with a knife.

5. Place the cellophane sheet on top of the wet tile.

6. Put trimmer on top of the cellophane and cut away any excess clay.

7. Place cardboard over the tile and release the wet tile by turning the mould upside down.

8. Remove cellophane sheet and lay cardboard on top.

Now set the tile aside to dry, still within the cardboard. The drying process should be slow, about three to four days.

When air dry, sponge edges and surface. Fire in kiln at 1020°C (1870°F).

4

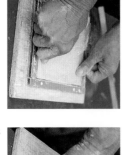

5

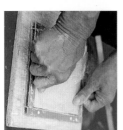

6

7

8

Requirements – painting

stain, in this case blue WMS 6339, and other colours as you wish

brushes: sleeper with fine point (see below)   tinter for shading – sable

liquid glaze

one glazed tile to mix stain

water

pencil or carbon paper

Draw the outline of your design onto the unglazed tile you wish to decorate using a pencil or carbon paper. This will fire away later, because it is organic.

Take one teaspoon of the powdery blue stain and mix it with a few drops of water until it is a smooth mix.

Load the sleeper brush with the watery paint and draw outlines of the design. After you have marked the outline, take the tinter brush and mix more water with the paint. The more water you use the lighter the colour blue will be.

Immediately dip the tile in the liquid glaze, shake off excess and fire tile in kiln at 1080°C (1970°F).

Note on sleeper brush

The sleeper brush is made from red squirrel hair. In Germany they call this brush the 'schlepper', in Holland they call it the 'trekker'. It is the most important tool in your painting. You have to cut it yourself with a good pair of small sharp scissors. Cut the hair around the middle and then try out your brush with paint. If the point is still too thick, cut a tiny bit more.

Remember that red squirrel hair is the only one suitable for this job. Sable hair is too soft.

Anke remembers that every Tuesday morning the painters of the Royal Delft Blue factory in the city of Delft were asked to view their work of the past week, still warm from the kiln. 'We always recognised each others touch by the way in which the sleeper was used'.

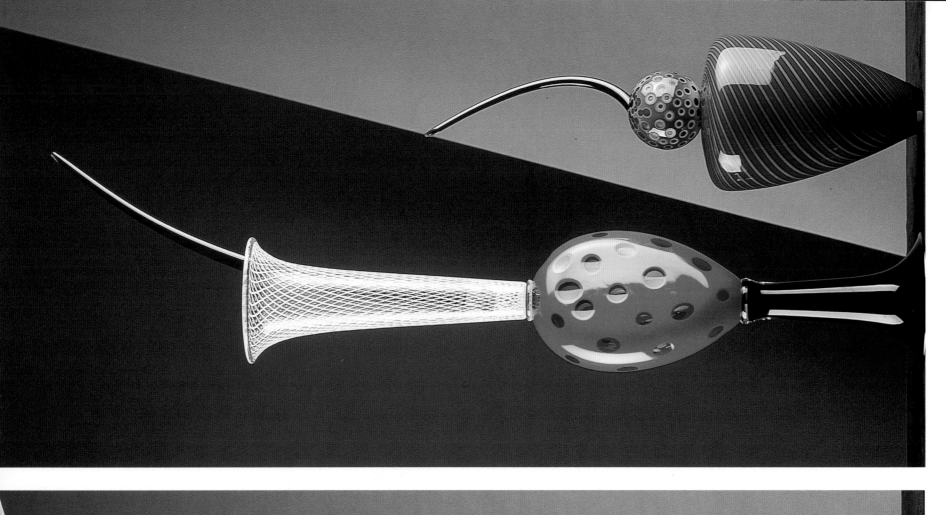

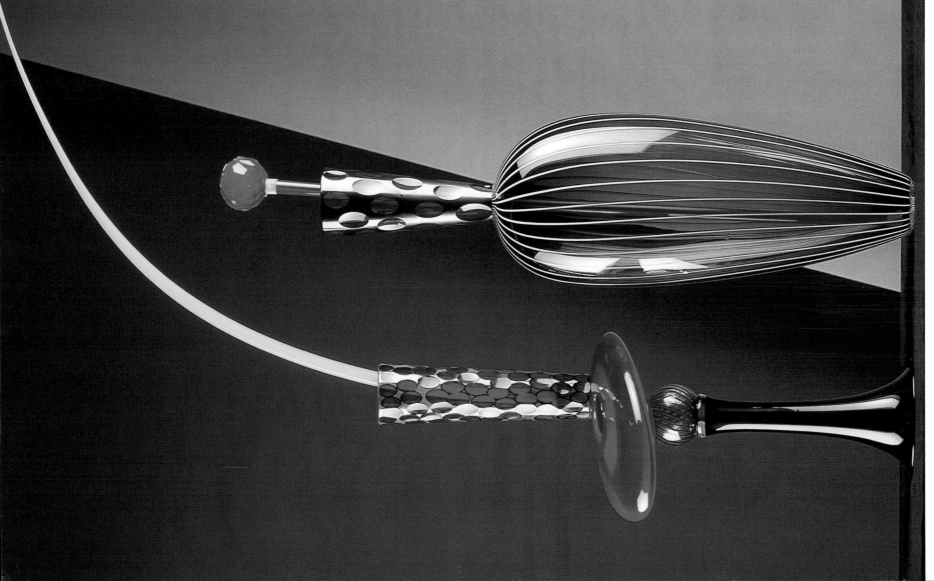

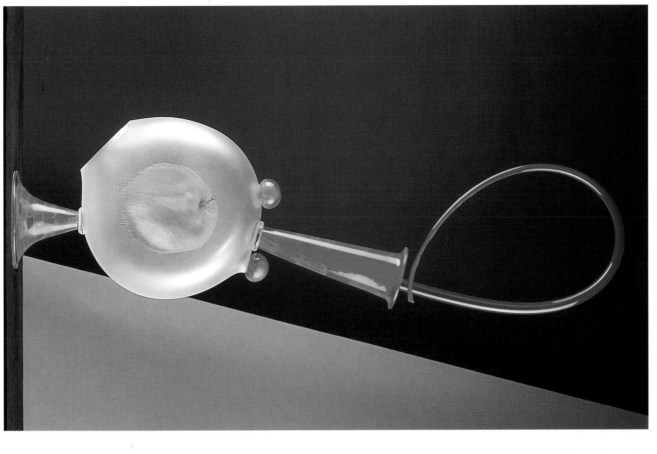

Scent Bottle

Nick Mount

One of the pioneers of glass art in Australia, Nick Mount has been working in the medium for almost 27 years. Throughout that time he has been pre-eminent in his field, exhibiting and teaching in Europe, South America, the United States and Japan. His commissions and prizes come from around the world. Two of the highlights of a long and illustrious career have been as a recipient of the Gold Medal, Bavarian State Prize, at Internationale Handwerksmesse, Munich, Germany in 1996 and receiving a Fellowship from the Visual Arts/Craft Fund of the Australia Council in 1999.

Nick's current work, the exquisite 'Scent bottle' series, refer in form and scale to a past tradition of creating large, highly decorated glass vessels which were used for display in apothecaries and perfumeries. Delicate yet striking, they display his virtuoso technique and his keen eye for fine design. Elegant and understated shapes are enhanced with striking colour and unusual details, or laminated together in seemingly random combinations.

Most of the blowing and colouring techniques Nick uses in his work are rooted in the traditions of Venetian glass. He enjoys working within the restrictions imposed by traditional furnace techniques, but also takes pleasure and excitement from selecting unrelated blown forms and joining them to create improbable compositions.

Nick Mount

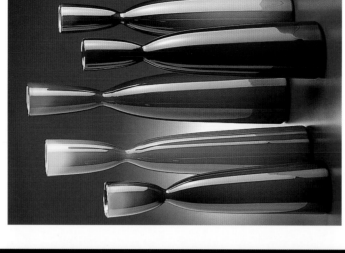
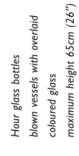

Hour glass bottles
blown vessels with overlaid
coloured glass
maximum height 65cm (26")

Blown bottles
surface finished, overlaid
colours
maximum height 65cm (26")

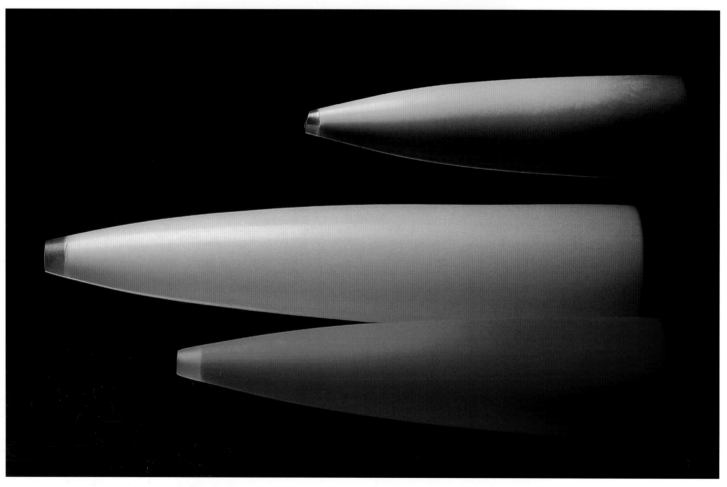

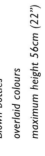
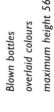

Blown bottles
overlaid colours
maximum height 56cm (22")

Elegant Blown Bottles

Elizabeth Kelly

Originally a trainee at the JamFactory Glass studio, of which she has been Head since 1997, Elizabeth Kelly went on to receive a B.A. in Visual arts at the Canberra Institute of the Arts, Australian National University, and then a Master of Visual Arts from Sydney College of the Arts, University of Sydney, where she also coordinated the hot glass programme and lectured for five years.

Established 27 years ago, JamFactory Contemporary Craft and Design in South Australia is a unique, integrated organisation for the design, production and sale of work by both leading and emerging Australian designer makers. Each of its design studios – glass, ceramics, metal and furniture – not only offers specialised knowledge of the design, development and manufacture of individual products, but also has the capacity to design and manufacture on a small to medium scale production run. They are also involved in producing commissioned work, taking this through all stages from design, prototype, manufacture and installation.

In her role at the JamFactory, Elizabeth works with the Design Associates, five in number at present. Approximately half of their time is spent working on JamFactory products and commissions, repairs, maintenance and general studio duties. The rest of the time is spent developing their own designed and articulated work which is then distributed through the JamFactory wholesale and retail outlets. These associates are recruited directly from universities around the country and they are provided with a bridging step towards professionalism. Elizabeth also organises national and international workshops in glass and regular, informal talks.

Elizabeth finds little time to produce her own beautiful, elegant and colourful bottles, which are widely recognised and have been exhibited worldwide, but she continues to develop her own designs while introducing new ideas at the Studio where she is currently incorporating computer-aided design into the production process.

Elizabeth Kelly

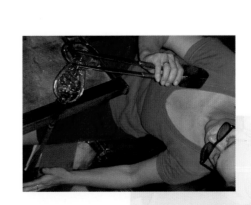

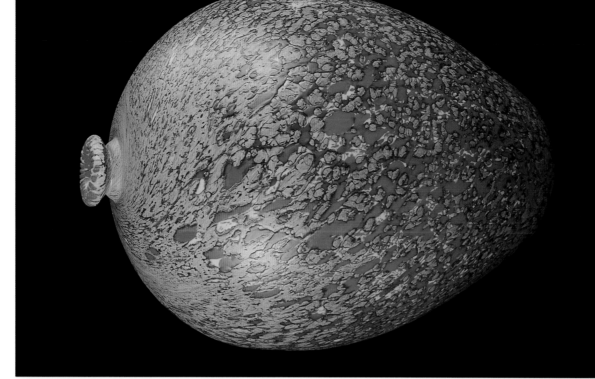

Phasmid vessel
blown glass
50cm high x 34cm diameter (20" x 13 1/2")

Phosphene moon
blown glass and cast bronze
70cm high x 52cm wide x 13cm (28" x 20 1/2" x 5")

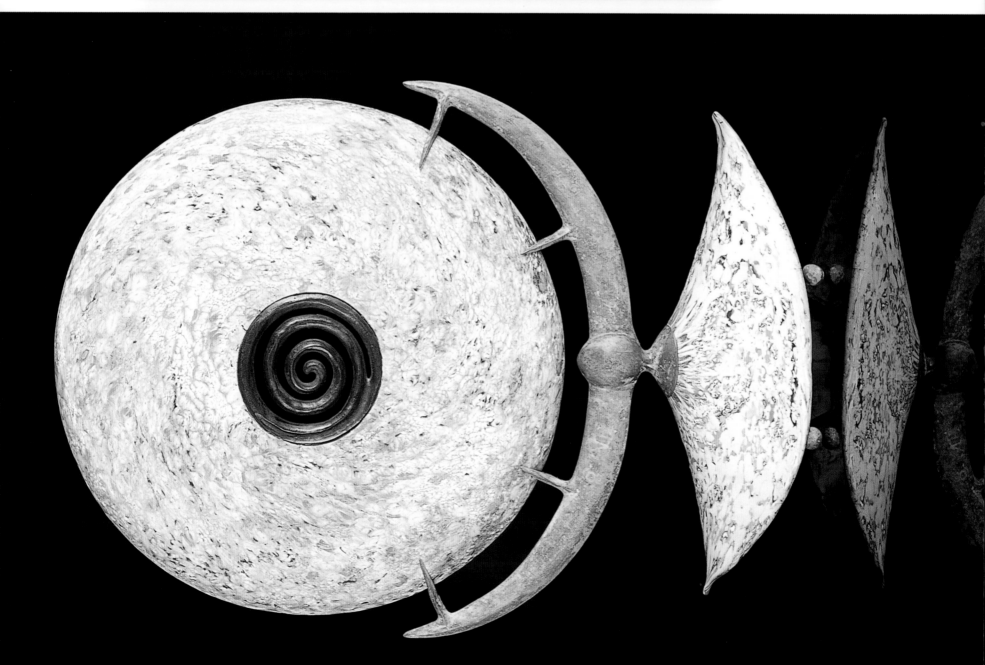

Vitrolith Glass

Colin Heaney

These works show Colin Heaney's great command of his art. Thirty years of experience and experimentation are contained in each piece of this magnificent glass, which reflect the colours of the ocean and the volcanic past of the land near his studio at Byron Bay, in northern New South Wales.

Colin had discovered many years ago the exciting effects the addition of metallic copper and bronze powders, combined with colour, could produce on glass. He experimented during quiet studio times to finally perfect his Vitrolith glass. The process is technically very difficult, variable and unpredictable, which makes the results even more enticing.

Colin works with a small team of assistants. It is backbreaking work and each piece takes several hours of constant attention, blowing, manipulation, colouring, all in close proximity to the glowing furnace. The molten glass is gathered on the blowpipe. Heaney selects colours and prepares the metallic powders, then the molten glass is rolled across these before being returned to the furnace. This might be repeated several more times with still more colour. And all the time the glass is being gently shaped at the end of the blowpipe.

Then the coloured glass is rolled in copper powder and returned to the heat, moved to a fume cupboard where more powdered glass is sprinkled on, then back to the fire for further heating and shaping, then more colours, and so on. The surface is cooled and blasted with blow torches to fuse extra colours, all the while being shaped on the blowpipe.

The final shaping is completed with the blowtorch and manipulation. Then more heat from the blowtorch and furnace and finally the glass is cracked off and placed in an annealing oven for **48** hours.

All the pieces are sandblasted to remove some of the oxides which form on the pieces as they are being created. In some pieces the oxide is left for aesthetic reasons, but they are still blasted to remove the gloss.

Finally, cast bronze is used in many pieces, but not all. A foundry professional works in close proximity to the glass studio and casts the pieces up to Colin Heaney's design. Sometimes a piece is preconceived to include the bronze, sometimes it is added quite a while after the glass is complete.

While this process seems demanding and exhausting, even more impressive is the ability of Colin to conceive of the whole before he begins the process, to visualise it, and to sustain this design through the arduous hours of work. His lengthy experience of the effects the colours and powders create, the aesthetics of these effects, as well as his enormous experience as a glass artist, allow him to complete his concepts to such perfection.

Colin Heaney

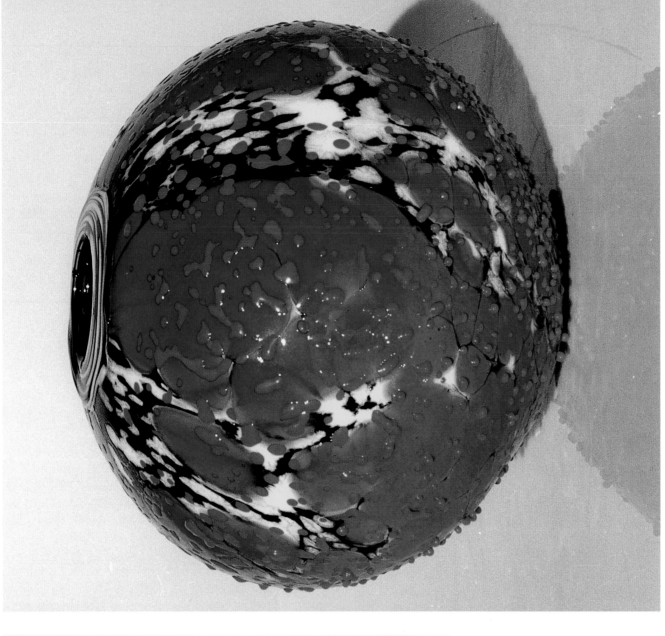

Hot chilli series (above left)
tall vase 28cm (11") high, sphere 14cm high x 16cm wide (5¹/₂" x 6¹/₄")

Coral scape (above right) 20cm (8") diameter

Iridised medium tulips and small jade bowl tulips (left) 18cm (7") and 14cm (5¹/₂") high

Sea Glass

John Lloyd and Geoff Murray

The sea, in all its life, colour and movement, is reflected in the sculptural and functional blown glass of John Lloyd and Geoff Murray of Lloyd Murray Glass.

Both men worked as blowers for Colin Heaney on the far north coast of New South Wales. After some years they decided to set up on their own in 1995 and built a glass blowing studio nearby.

With a collective experience of more than 16 years working with hot glass, they have the confidence, the skills, timing and, above all, the balance of control and spontaneity necessary to create good glass.

From the initial gather of hot glass, through decorating and forming, they work with each other, alternating between maker and assistant, and it is the combination of their individual styles which creates the successful interplay of ideas, colours and forms.

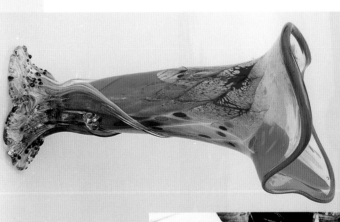

Pink lady freeform vase
34cm high x 18cm wide at top
(13 1/2" x 7")

Pink lady platter
22cm high x 46cm wide
(8 1/2" x 18")

John Lloyd

Geoff Murray

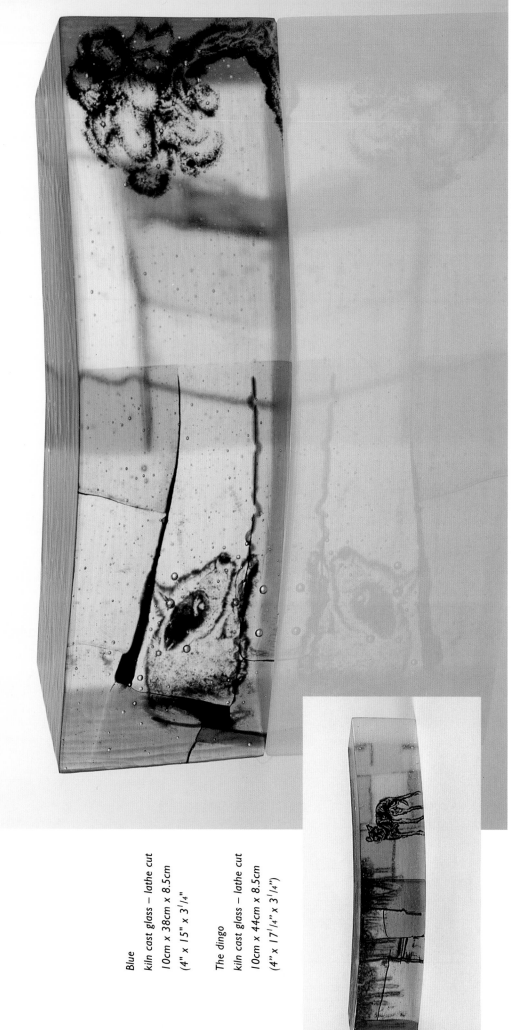

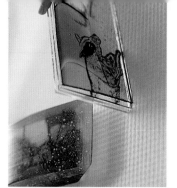

Blue
kiln cast glass – lathe cut
10cm x 38cm x 8.5cm
(4" x 15" x 3¹/4")

The dingo
kiln cast glass – lathe cut
10cm x 44cm x 8.5cm
(4" x 17¹/4" x 3¹/4")

Kirstie Rea

T
he recent works of Kirstie Rea are abstract panoramic landscapes in glass. Very Australian in their colour and intensity of light, and reflecting the broadness of the land, each is given a specific, literal, locating imagery such as a eucalyptus or pencil pine at the front gate.

Originally working in stained glass, Kirstie then attended and later was a part-time lecturer at the prestigious Canberra Institute of the Arts Glass Workshop. She is recognised worldwide for her innovative designs and methods and has twice been artist-in-residence at the Bullseye Glass Company in Portland, Oregon, as well as other institutions both in Australia and overseas.

Kirstie is a kiln worker and her works are, in the main, kiln formed, although she works with a blower at one important stage of the process.

A   Three layers of different sizes and colours of glass are fused together in the kiln at 820°C to make a large tile. In this way Kirstie creates her own, new and individual colour palette.

B   Then the tile is reheated, rolled and blown into a vase shape. This changes the colour and intensity of light in the glass.

C   The base of the vase shape is cut off with a diamond wheel and the side of the vase is scored before it is replaced into the kiln where it flattens out again.

D   This flattened glass is then scored freehand and broken into smaller pieces with running pliers.

E   On plain, clear glass Kirstie draws her 'literal' images – trees, dogs, horses. These are drawn freehand with black glass powder using the blunt end of a brush or a scalpel to sharpen the lines.

G

Plain glass is placed either side of these images, then layers of plain and coloured glass, as previously prepared, are added around the image. Up to 20 layers of glass can be added.

F   This layered glass is fused together in the kiln at 840°C (1500°F) then cut on a lathe and ground on a grinder while flat.

The fused glass is then slumped in a kiln at 635°C (1175°F).

G   For the larger works Kirstie uses a large stainless steel form to shape the glass in the kiln to create the curve of her panoramic landscapes.

Kirstie Rea

Baroque shaped crystal opal
specimen from Andamooka set in
18 carat gold
1.5cm x 1.7cm ($^5/_8$" x $^3/_4$")

White and grey Broome pearls,
matched with blue aquamarines and
a blister pearl brooch

Marylyn Verstraeten

J ewellery making follows two major streams, constructed or cast. Marylyn Verstraeten casts her jewellery, and creates small, realistic creatures or flora.

Marylyn has travelled long distances in Australia, intrigued by the landscape and by bird and animal life. Vast stores of images have resulted. She has created a series of flora and fauna, such as the Silver skink darting from a hole in an organza gumleaf. She also likes to design jewellery around baroque pearl shapes and prefers to work with opal, sapphire and other typically Australian gems. There may be Broome pearls blended with the seagreen of the Australian boulder opal reminiscent of the Indian Ocean, or sculptured Australian opal and pearl rings with soft greens and the ochre of outback colours.

After repeated requests from specialist collectors, Marylyn also designs a series of silver thimbles decorated with Australian motifs.

In cast jewellery a piece of solid wax is cold-carved or hot-sculpted into shape with heated modelling scalpels. Once work on the wax model is finished, a 'sprue' or feeder tube is attached to one corner of the model and the sprued wax model is then suspended in a circular metal container filled with plaster.

When the plaster has set and the metal cylinder is heated to red hot, the wax evaporates, or is 'lost', through the feeder tube. This then leaves a cavity into which the silver can be poured. The result is a perfect replica of the wax model, but this time in precious metal. In silversmiths' parlance the process is logically referred to as 'lost wax casting'. Marylyn uses this method, with some minor variations.

Making a thimble - short production run

1. The starting point is to carve a completely finished metal 'master' in silver. This master is suspended in a small rectangular upright container. The container is filled with liquid silicon rubber which will form a mould around the thimble. When the rubber has set the mould is carefully cut in half in an irregular zig zag fashion and the master lifted out.

2. The zig zag cut allows the two halves of the mould to be keyed together again precisely, leaving a thimble shape cavity in the middle. A small feeder channel or 'sprue' is cut from the cavity to the top of the mould. This allows heated liquid wax to be shot into the cavity under pressure and the result is a hard wax copy of the silver thimble. This process allows a number of identical 'waxes' to be made.

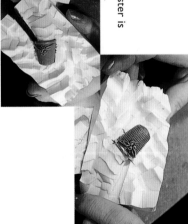

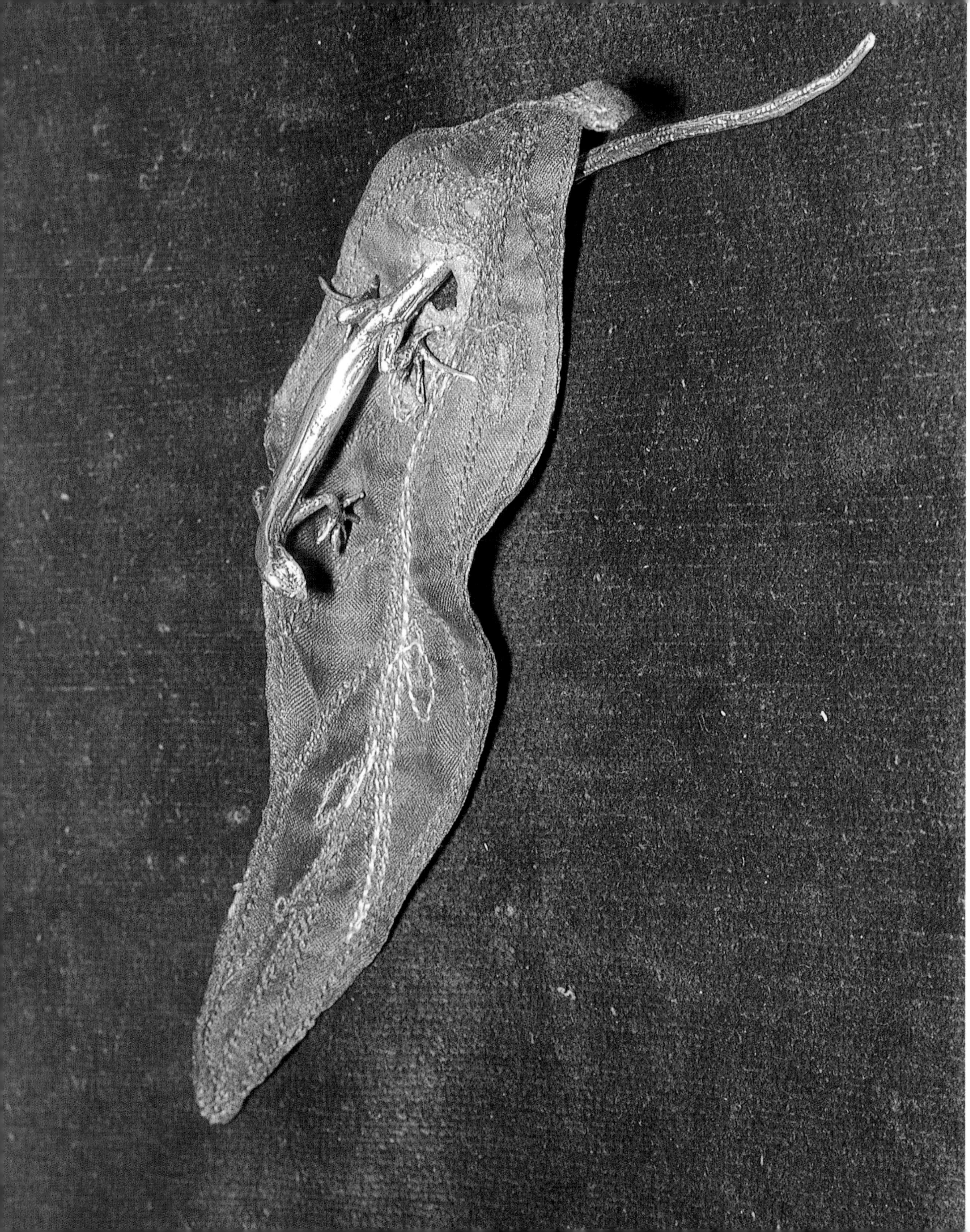

3. The wax model is now further worked on to give each thimble its own individuality. At this stage, too, the gumnut motive shown here could be completely removed and an altogether different design sculpted in its place. This new wax pattern then could in turn form the basis for an entirely different metal master.

4. The wax model, complete with a sprue re-attached is suspended in a circular metal container filled with plaster. When the plaster has set the metal cylinder is heated to red hot. The wax evaporates and vents out through the sprue hole. Silver, heated to a liquid, can now be poured in and the result is a perfect silver replica of the wax model. Then the sprue is sawn off.

5. Then Marylyn finishes the thimble. The remainder of the sprue is carefully filed away and the small details enhanced with fine chisels and a flexible drive with fast spinning mini abrasive discs in its handpiece. Marylyn later acid-stains the thimble dark to add character and polishes the highlights.

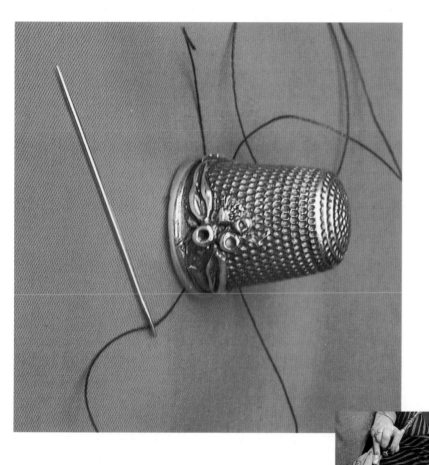

Right: Thimble with
gum leaf motif
3cm (1¹/₄")

Left: Skink in
sterling silver
darting through
organza gum leaf
14cm (5¹/₂") long

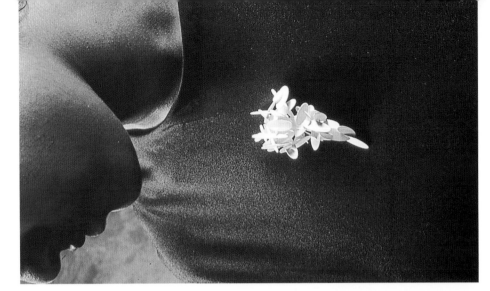

Nimrod brooch
925 silver
7cm x 4cm x 1.8cm
(2³/₄" x 1¹/₂" x ⁵/₈")

Wreath brooch
925 silver
6cm (2¹/₂") diameter x 2cm (³/₄")

Chaotic brooch
750 gold
7cm x 4cm x 1.8cm
(2³/₄" x 1¹/₂" x ⁵/₈")

Silver and Gold Jewels

Rowena Gough

O ld mother-of-pearl buttons have featured in much of Rowena Gough's recent jewellery. Strung together to form stunning bandoliers and necklaces, on one level these reflected her fascination in and knowledge of Pacific culture, being reminiscent, for example, of shell money, and their fragility resonating like the tenuousness of the traditional cultures. On another level they celebrated the value of women's work, made for women as stunning and sensuous decoration while constructed of buttons, symbols of their domestic history and role.

In the pieces shown here, Rowena has moved on to create her own beautiful white discs, as she was frustrated with the fragility of the pearl shell and her difficulty in slicing and connecting it. In silver, and some gold, she has recreated the reflective qualities of the shell and extended the shape to an ellipse. The brooches show her fascination with geometry, structure, spatial relationships and patterning.

Rowena melts small pieces of silver into a ball and then these are repeatedly cold rolled through a mill to form the elliptical shape. Each disc is approximately 5mm × 7mm ($^1/_4$" × $^1/_3$").

The flat surfaces are cleaned with emery paper and then the discs are sliced part way through with a jeweller's piercing saw.

They can then be slotted into each other. Two or three are slotted together at a time, placed to form a pleasing pattern, and to create an interplay of light and shade. Each small group is soldered carefully together before another group is constructed. Gradually all are formed together into a larger pattern.

The whole is repetitively heated, cooled and placed in dilute acid solution to develop a thick coat of fine silver on the surface. This may be done six, eight or ten times and scours the copper oxide from the surface.

Then the edges are burnished to a high polish, leaving the faces white. A platform is added to the back of the brooch for the fitting.

This is painstaking, grinding, grimy and aching work, yet it results in delicate, feminine forms where light and shadow play on their myriad surfaces.

Artists' Biographies

Anke Arkesteyn 122
Delft Blue Pottery
Boronia, Vic.
Born Delft, Holland
In Australia since 1983
Studied: trained as ceramic painter at well known establishment in Delft; graduated in Graphic Art at Academy of Fine Art Enschede, Holland.
Related experience: ceramic painter in Delft; daily demonstrations at Royal factory 'de Porcelaine Fles' in Delft; teacher in music-dance and fine art; accomplished harpist; established Delft Blue Pottery 1985. Awards and exhibitions: numerous exhibitions in Delft and Australia; work displayed at Rembrandt Connection, Melbourne and Delft Blue Pottery.

Jennifer Bennell 59
Sydney, NSW
Born Crib Point, Vic.
Studied: Decorative painted finishes with Gael Laurence and Joanne Day at Laurence/Day Studios, San Francisco 1982-83.
Related experience: Operated studio, The Painted Finish, in Sydney, working on commissions and teaching, 1984-97; Manufacturer of mediums and paints for the industry under the Jennifer Bennell Magic Effects label.
Teaching experience: Taught full time at studio, Painted Finish, in Sydney 1984-97; lecturer in the history of lacquer, gilding, paint finishes.
Publications: Books Master Strokes, Master Works (Random House), Painted Finishes; numerous magazine articles and projects.

Sandra Black 103
Perth, WA
Born Bairnsdale, Vic. 1950
Studied: Teaching, Claremont Teachers' College and Nedlands Secondary Teachers' College, 1968-70.
Teaching experience: secondary teacher, Education Department of WA 1971-75; part time lecturer in Ceramics WA Institute of Technology 1975-79; part time lecturer Mt Lawley College of Advanced Education, WA (now Edith Cowan University) 1979; full time lecturer Bendigo College of Advanced Education, Vic. 1984; part time lecturer Faculty of Art, Edith Cowan University 1987-93; part time lecturer, Ceramics, Curtin University, WA 1989-90; part time lecturer Ceramics Central Metropolitan College TAFE, St Brigids, 1994-98; part time lecturer Carine TAFE 1996-99; various part time lectureships and visiting artist positions, including Ceramic Workshop, Canberra School of Art 1982; Sydney College of Arts 1983; School of Art, University of Tas. 1985; Royal Melbourne Institute of Technology 1991; various workshops and lecture tours including NT 1985; NZ 1988, 1990; USA 1991; NSW Ceramic Study Group, Macquarie University 1997; Canada 1997.
Related experience: Member Visual Arts & Crafts Panel, WA Department for the Arts; Vice President Crafts Council of WA.
Exhibitions and awards: numerous solo and group exhibitions and awards including most recently: solo: Perth Galleries, Perth 1998; Distelfink Gallery, Melbourne 1998; group: Global Ceramics 1, Babel Gallery, Amsterdam 1998; Southern Light, SOFA, USA 1998; National Craft Acquisition Award, Museum and Art Gallery of the NT 1995
Collections: numerous including: National Gallery of Australia;

Canberra Parliament House Art Collection, Canberra; state and regional art galleries throughout Australia; Powerhouse Museum, Sydney; Toki Ceramic Research Institute, Japan; Universities including Edith Cowan; Melbourne, Southern Qld, Curtin; Australia Japan Foundation, Tokyo; Gifhu Prefecture Ceramic Museum, Tajimi City, Japan; Auckland Institute and Museum.

Les Blakebrough 107
Hobart, Tas.
Born Surrey, England 1930
In Australia since 1948
Studied: apprenticed to Ivan McMeekin, Sturt Pottery, Mittagong, NSW 1957-59; studied with Takeichi Kawai, Kyoto, Japan 1963-64; Churchill Fellowship to Europe 1992; research study at major porcelain factories in Scandinavia and UK 1993.
Related experience: manager Sturt Pottery, Mittagong 1969-72; Director, Sturt Craft Centre, Mittagong 1964-72; foundation member, Crafts Board, Australia Council 1973-77; Senior lecturer and Head, Ceramics Department, Tas. School of Art 1973-81; Private workshop Mt Nelson, Tas. 1974; 1st judge International Fletcher Brownbuilt Award, Auckland, NZ 1978; Associate Professor and Head, Ceramic Studio, University of Tas. 1989-94; Established Ceramics Research Unit, University of Tas. 1990; Principal Research Fellow, Ceramic Research Unit, University of Tas. 1996 – .
Exhibitions and awards: numerous including recent solo: Savode Gallery, Brisbane, Qld 1997; Ceramic Art Gallery, Paddington, NSW 1997; BMG Fine Art, Adelaide, SA 1998; BMG Fine Art 2000; recent group: Four Visions of Antarctica, Newcastle City Gallery 1997; Contemporary Australian Craft to Japan/Hokkaido-Takaoka-Shiga+Sydney NSW Custom House 1999; recent awards: Sidney Myer Ceramic Award/Exhibition, Shepparton, Vic. 1996; Newcastle City Gallery Ceramic Purchase Award 1996.
Publications: author and/or subject of numerous articles in magazines, journals and books, including: Ceramics Technical; Ceramics Art & Perception; Craft Arts.
Collections: numerous including: National Gallery of Australia, Canberra; Admiralty House, Sydney; Australian Embassy, Beijing, China; Commonwealth Collection, London; Imperial Palace Collection, Tokyo, Japan; International Museum of Ceramic Art, Firenza, Italy; Universities of Tas., Flinders, Qld, WA; all Australian State Galleries.

Stephen Bowers 117
Adelaide, SA
Born Katoomba NSW 1952
Studied: Diploma of Teaching, Alexander Mackie College of Advanced Education, Sydney 1971-73; Diploma of art (Stage 2), National Art School, Darlinghurst, Sydney 1974-76; Bachelor of Education, Underdale College of Advanced Education, Adelaide 1984-86.
Teaching experience: (recent) Lill Street Studios, Chicago 1995; International Ceramic Exhibition, Faenza, Italy 1995; Queensbury Hunt Design Group, London 1995; SOFA, Chicago 1996; Escola Massana Barcelona Espana 1997; Ceramics Festive, Artists Residency and Exhibition, Gubbio, Italy 1999.
Related experience: Head of Ceramics JamFactory Craft and Design Centre 1990-1999; Member Visual Arts, Crafts and Design Advisory Committee of the SA Department for the Arts and Cultural Development 1989-91, Chair 1991-92; Member Craft Council of SA, Education Committee 1990-91; Crafts Council of S A 1989-96; Senior Development Officer Arts SA 1999 – .
Exhibitions and awards: (recent) more than 40 group touring and

national survey exhibitions in Australia; International survey exhibitions and expositions in Britain, Japan, Thailand, Hong Kong, Indonesia, China, USA, Italy, Singapore and Scotland; National Craft Acquisition award, Alice Springs 1996.
Commissions and collections: major design and manufacture commissions for the Government of SA including the Premier's Department at JamFactory 1997; Art works at Morphett Street Bridge, Adelaide City Council 1999; public and private collections including state and regional galleries, Australian National Gallery, Canberra, Powerhouse Museum, Sydney, Janet Holmes à Court Collection, Kumagai (Australian) Collection, National Museum of History, Taipei, Taiwan.

Pat Dale 93

Leongatha, Vic.

Born 1938

Studied: Diploma of Visual arts, Gippsland Institute of Education (now Monash University, Gippsland Campus); Douglas Fuchs Workshop, Melbourne 1982; Fijian Basket Makers, Fiji 1986; conference 'Reeds and Baskets' Melbourne 1986; conference workshop with Tori de Mestre 1997; painting with US tutors 1992, 95, 97; willow basketry, NZ tutor 1008; Apache Indian basketry, New Mexico, USA 1999.

Teaching and related experience: Australian Craft Show, Canberra 1994; Adult Education (basketry and decorative painting) Sydney, Qld and Vic. 1982- ; Arts Access, Bairnsdale (basketry) 1988; coordinated exhibitions at Seniwati Women's Gallery, Bali 1995, 99; private tutor to students of decorative painting 1989- ; cultural tour leader annual trip to Indonesia 1987- .

Exhibitions and awards: solo exhibitions Artworks Gallery, Nungurner 1992, 94; Baskets, Australia and Bali, Seniwati Gallery, Bali, Indonesia 1996; Basketry in the Southern Hills, Leongatha 1999; Vineyards and Gardens, Coal Creek Gallery, Korumburra, Vic. 1999.

Publications: author book Basketry and weaving with Natural Materials 1998.

Jane Devine 49

Hawthorn, Vic.

Born Dubbo, NSW 1944

Studied: Secondary arts and crafts 1961-64; Prahran Technical College; Royal Melbourne Institute of Technology; Fine Arts, Melbourne University; Carpet making and design, Boston 1974; Period furniture decoration and textile design, London 1975-76; Watercolour painting, Vic. Artists Society 1988-90.

Teaching experience: Vic. secondary schools 1965-73; Summer school, textile decoration, Melbourne University 1990-98.

Exhibitions and awards: solo, private 1987, 89, 91, 94; Reflections Gallery 1997; Australian Scholarship Group Centennial Artist 2000.

Publications: author book Embellished 1997; illustrator Susan Dickens' The Art of Tassel Making 1994 and Tassels 2000.

Pippin Drysdale 109

Perth, WA

Born Melbourne 1943

Studied (and Honorifics): Diploma Advanced Ceramics, Perth Technical College (WA School of Art and design) 1982; Bachelor of Arts (Fine art), WA Institute of Technology (Curtin University) 1986; Adjunct Research Fellow, School of Art, Curtin University of Technology 1997-; Fellow of Craftwest 1994 - .

Teaching, workshops and residencies: study tour USA - Anderson Ranch, Colorado, associate potter Rhoda Lopez Clay Dimensions, San Diego 1982; guest lecturer, School of Art, University of Tas., Hobart 1988; Artist in Residence 1991; Swansea Art College, Wales, Deruta Grazia Maioliche Pottery, Perugia, Italy; cultural exchange Artists' Union of Russia, Tomsk University, Siberia 1991; guest lecturer: Princeton University, Skidmore College, Boise State University, Washington State University 1991; artist in residence and visiting lecturer Canberra School of Art, Canberra 1994; guest lecturer, Washington State University, Seattle 1994; national tour Master Workshops and lectures Australia 1996; guest lecturer Auckland Studio Potters Summer School, NZ 1997; Master Workshops national tour for NZ Society of Potters, NZ; Field trip to NT as part of ArtsWA Fellowships 1998; International Lustre Symposium, Gubbio, Italy.

Exhibitions: (recent solo including) Beaver Galleries, Canberra 1997; Distelfink Galleries, Melbourne 1997; Pots on Ponsonby, Auckland, NZ 1997; Perth Galleries 1999; Quadrivium, Sydney 2000; (recent group, fairs and expos): SOFA New York and Chicago 1998; numerous group exhibitions in Australia, Italy, USA, NZ, Singapore.

Commissions and collections: gift for Mr and Mrs G. Whitlam 1987; presentation pieces for Department of Prime Minister and Cabinet 1988-89; Department of Trade and Development 1990; Murdoch Collection 1994; Perth College 1995; Port Hedland Centenary 1996; St. Hilda's School Centennial commemorative porcelain bowls 1996; Grain Pool of WA presentation for Seoul, Korea 1997; represented in all state and regional galleries; National Gallery of Australia; university collections; Powerhouse Museum, Sydney; Artbank; Tomsk State Gallery and Museum, Siberia; Novosirbirsk State Gallery, Siberia; Attorney general's office, WA; numerous private collections.

Nancy Duggan 89

Woodville, SA

Born Adelaide 1940

Studied: Art Craft Certificate, Marleston College of Wool and Textiles 1983.

Teaching experience: 1986-99 including recently Kangaroo Island Adult Education 1997; Flinders Fibre School; Melrose 1998; Basketmakers of Vic. 1999, 2000.

Exhibitions and awards: selected group exhibitions including: Floating Forest and Australian Basketry (Douglas Fuchs), Meat Market Craft Centre, Vic. 1982; Basketry and bush furniture, Distelfink Gallery, Melbourne 1984; Quaint Dreaming, JamFactory Craft and Design Centre, Adelaide 1987; Language of Form, Craftspace, The Rocks, Sydney 1993; Links - reconciliation exhibition, Prospect Gallery, SA 1999; Gathering '99 Lismore; Look at me now - Basketmakers of Vic., Glen Eira City Gallery, Melbourne 2000.

Collections: Vic. State Craft Collection; National Gallery of Australia; Craft Council of NT, Alice Springs; Art Gallery of SA.

Beverley Evans 21

McKellar Découpage

Gold Coast, Qld

Born Maitand, NSW 1941

Studied: Decoupage with Nerida Singleton

Exhibitions and awards: Bell Gallery, Boweal, NSW; Fine Arts Exhibition 1994; Sue Ellen's Antique Gallery, Gold Coast; Galerie Mason Et Jardin, Sanctuary Cove, Gold Coast; Platypus Gallery, Village Square, Gold Coast; Summer House, Noosa Heads, Qld; Benny and The Bears Gallery, Sydney, NSW; Lexus Centre, Brisbane; Seven awards at Découpage Guild of Australia Exhibition 1996; First prize with Middle Eastern Style Briefcase, Norton Bay College Festival on the Bay Art Exhibition 1999.

Rowena Gough 139
Melbourne, Vic.
Born Maryborough, Vic. 1958
Studied: Diploma of Art (Design), Gold and Silversmithing, Royal Melbourne Institute of Technology 1978; Bachelor of Education, Melbourne State College 1980; Master of Visual Arts, Sydney College of the Arts, University of Sydney 1988.
Teaching experience: lecturer, Jewellery and Object Design Studio, Sydney College of the Arts, University of Sydney 1989-96; seminar programme for European Metals Exhibition, Powerhouse Museum, Sydney 1990-92; public lectures on Contemporary Jewellery in Australia and NZ 1990-92; Masterclass Lecturer, Jewellery and Silversmithing Department, Royal College of Art, London 1999.
Related experience: Board Member, Vice President Centre for Contemporary Crafts 1993-96; editorial committee, 'Object' magazine 1994-96; Jewellers and Metalsmiths Group of Australia Conferences 1980 (initiating member), 82, 84, 86, 88, 92, 95; member board Crafts Council of Vic. 1982-83.
Exhibitions: (solo, recent): Finger Gallery, Auckland, NZ and Fluxus Gallery, Dunedin, NZ 1996; 'White Heart, Dark Truths, Deep Waters, Soulful Dreaming' Crawford Gallery, Sydney 1997; (group, recent): numerous including National Museum of Scotland, Edinburgh 1999; Galerie Ra, Amsterdam 1998; Itamia City Craft centre; Ueno no Mori Museum, Tokyo 1998; Hokkaido Museum of Modern Art, Takaoka City art Museum, Museum of Modern Art, Shiga, Japan 1999; Lesley Craze Gallery, London 2000.
Commissions and collections: Emeritus Medals, Visual Arts Crafts Board of the Australia Council 1994 and 95; National Gallery of Australia, regional and state galleries of Australia, RMIT, Melbourne, Vic. Education Department, Powerhouse Museum, Sydney; Museum fur Kunsthandwerk, Frankfurt, Germany; Neue Sammlung, Munich Germany; Galerie Ra Collection, Amsterdam, Netherlands

Judy Grey-Gardner 94
Alice Springs, NT
Born SA 1933
Studied: fibre basketry with the Fibre Basket Weavers of SA Inc 1989; attended workshops in Adelaide and Mittagong, NSW, on a variety of techniques; involved in indigenous basketmakers conference attended by Aboriginal basketmakers from all states and several First Nation groups from California, Camp Coorong, SA 1996.
Teaching experience: has conducted workshops on a variety of basketry techniques.
Related experience: President of Fibre Basket Weavers of SA, Inc 1994, 95, 99; member organising committee for the Biennial Basketry Conference in Adelaide 1995.
Exhibitions: numerous group displays and exhibitions including: (Adelaide galleries) Yannahee Gallery, Prospect Gallery, Hughes Gallery, Fullarton, Box Factory, Pepper Street Gallery and SA Museum Shop; Waikerie, SA, Springton, SA, Barossa Valley, SA; galleries in Gold Coast, Alice Springs, Sydney, Lismore, Bali.
Collections: numerous private collections in SA, Qld, Vic., NSW and USA as well as Mitcham Council in SA.

Margôt Hamilton 25
Sassafras, Vic.
Born Melbourne 1943
Studied: Decoupage, Council of Adult Education, Melbourne 1993; Decoupage, gilding, furniture painting, Malmesbury, England 1996; Italian language, Florence, Italy 1996.
Teaching experience: Council of Adult Education and private classes, tutor in decoupage 1995-98.
Awards and exhibitions: solo exhibition, Vic. Arts Centre 1997.

Geoffrey Hannah 75
Lismore, NSW
Born 1948
Studied: apprenticeship in cabinet making from 1963; Churchill Fellowship researching fine furniture form the period 1635-1850 throughout England and France 1980.
Related experience: established own workshop and business in 1973.
Teaching experience: runs furniture making classes from own workshop and tutors in furniture making, restoration and marquetry throughout Australia including the Australian National University, McGregor Summer School, Artlink, Arts West and private organisations.
Exhibitions and awards: has participated in numerous joint exhibitions both local and interstate, as well as solo exhibitions; last major work, Australiana Collectors' Cabinet has been touring capital and major cities; Silver Medallion for the Arts in Lismore's Australia Day awards 1988; won Traditional Furniture section of National Woodwork Exhibition Melbourne for four consecutive years.
Collections: many private and public collections including Australiana Fund purchase for residence of Governor General in Canberra.
Publications: numerous articles in magazines, journals and books.

Lorraine Hansen 119
Melbourne, Vic.
Born Melbourne
Studied: trained as a florist; TAFE training, porcelain studies with Amy Lakides, June Ling, Jean Gillespie and Nance Graham; with Milwyn Holloway - Worcester; with Gerald Delaney - Worcester style fruit; with John McLaughlin - Royal crown Derby; watercolour studies with Alvaro Castagnet, Joseph Zbukvic and Ron Muller.
Teaching experience: a teacher for 32 years; runs private workshops and classes from own studio and at commercial venues throughout Australia; qualified TAFE teacher; member Australasian Porcelain Art Teachers (Vic. branch); member of Vic. branch of International Porcelain Art Teachers Associations of the USA; has demonstrated in USA.
Related experience: founding member of Vic. Guild of China Painters and now Life Member; member International Porcelain Association; member Vic. Artists Society; featured artist Wedgwood Society 1983, 84; ran school at IPAT Convention Melbourne 1985; featured artist

SAPAT Association Adelaide 1994 and 95; judge of Royal Melbourne Show (4 years), Dandenong Show, Warragul Show and Bendigo Show 1994, 95, 96 and 99.

Exhibitions and awards: solo and with others: numerous including most recent at Australian National Flower Show 1994-2000; Meat Market Craft Centre 1996; Rose Week 99; third prize International Porcelain Painters' Convention, Minneapolis 1990.

Colin Heaney 129

Colin Heaney Hot Glass
Byron Bay, NSW

Born Vancouver, Canada 1948
Settled in California, USA 1956
Arrived in Australia 1967

Basically self-taught; started first glass-blowing studio in 1982 and experimented.

Exhibitions and awards:: recent selected: 46 Australian and international exhibitions 1983-97; Raglan Gallery, Sydney (solo) 1998; Raglan Gallery SOFA New York and Chicago 1998; RFC Glass Prize, Touring exhibition 1998; Glass Invitational, Emerald City Fine Art, Seattle, USA 1998; Habatat Gallery, Boca Raton, Florida USA 1999; Habatat Gallery, Chicago 1999; Raglan Gallery, SOFA, Chicago 1999; Framed Gallery, Darwin 1999; Art and Design Gallery, Brisbane 1999; Glass Invitational, Emerald City Fine Art, Seattle 1999; Ausglass Members Exhibition, Wagga Wagga Art Gallery 1999; Institute of Nuclear Technology, Lisbon, Portugal 1999; Craft Qld Gallery, Brisbane 1999; Glass Canvas Gallery, St Petersburg, Florida 1999; University of Technology 1999; Gallery L, Hamburg, Germany (solo); Rachael Collection, Aspen, USA (solo); Habatat Gallery, Detroit, USA; SOFA New York; MG 1999 Award, Mostly Glass Gallery, Eaglewood, New Jersey USA.

Collections: private and public collections throughout Australia, Germany, Singapore, USA, Channel Islands, UK, Canada, Italy, Bali, Spain, Hong Kong, Monaco, France, U.A.E., Israel, Ireland including Corning Museum of Glass, New York and Ebeltoft Glasmuseum, Denmark.

Robert Howard 85

Beaumont, NSW

Born Stanthorpe, Qld

Studied: Bachelor of Engineering (Hons), University of NSW 1966-71.
Related experience: studio woodworker 1988 - ; president Sydney Woodcarvers Group 1996-98; Vice President Woodworkers Association of NSW 1997-98; judge Oberon Wood Exhibition 1996; contributor 'Australian Wood Review' 1996 - .

Exhibitions and awards: (selected recent): Australian Craft Show, Sydney 1989-98; 'Wood at the Rocks', Craftspace Gallery, Sydney 1995; Bowral Craft Expo, Bowral NSW 1996-97; Glenaeon Craft Expo, Middle Cove, NSW 1996-98; Bega Wood Exhibitions, Bega NSW 1996 (awarded second prize for sculpture); National Wood Exhibition 1997; 'Working with Wood' Show, Sydney, NSW 1997; People's Choice Award, Oberon Wood Exhibition, Oberon NSW, 1997; First prize Traditional Furniture, National Wood Competition 1997; 'Presiding Officers' Craft Prize', New Parliament House, Canberra 1999.

Ann Johnston 41

Cluny Studio Workshop
Concord, NSW

Born Sydney 1944

Studied: Fine Arts, National Art School, Sydney, Teachers Guild of NSW.
Teaching experience: London, Toronto, Canada 1966-68; secondary school art teaching 1968-77; Head Visual Arts Department, Our Lady of Mercy College, Parramatta 1978; teacher of Decorative Arts at own Cluny Studio Workshop, Concord, NSW 1993 - ; visiting teacher, country NSW, other states and USA.
Publications: book Mediaeval Folk in Painting; magazine articles and projects.
Recent commissions: Large trompe l'oeil mural at Milton Park, Bowral 1999.

Adrian Hunt 77

The Deepings
Deepings, Tas.

Born Sydney 1933

Studied: University of Sydney - B.Sc. (Gen. Sci), Diploma in Education 1959; Sydney Technical College - Woodturning 1981.
Teaching experience: Teacher of secondary school science for 24 years in NSW including some work with TAFE Colleges; Science Master, Ascham, Edgecliff, Sydney 1973-82; woodturning tuition, one to one, beginners to master class 1990 - .

Exhibitions and awards: Crafts Council of Tas. and Tas. Wood Design Collection exhibitions.
Commissions: Anglican Diocese of Tas. - four blackwood standing candlesticks and two sets of alter candlesticks, all for St David's Cathedral, Hobart 1998; Arts Tas. Art for Public Buildings Scheme - outdoor chess set and board.
(See also Jill Roberts)

Emily Hurt 83

Canberra, ACT

Born Boston, USA 1939
Arrived Australia 1962

Studied: Bachelor of Arts, Randolph-Macon Women's College, USA 1960.

Experience: art design, woodcraft - all self-taught.
Exhibitions: regular exhibition at Bungendore Woodworks Gallery, Bungendore, NSW.
Collections: numerous private collections throughout Australia

'Contemporary Wood from an Ancient Land', SOFA, Chicago 1999.
Collection and commissions: St George Private Hospital; Robert M. Bohlen Collection, USA; Warwick Collection, USA; Allan and Joy Nachman Collection, USA; private collections in Australia, Holland, France, Korea and Japan.

Virginia Kaiser 87
Beaumont, NSW

Studied: Art and Craft Certificate (incomplete) Marleston and Norwood TAFE, SA 1976-77; Handweaving I, School of Textiles, Strathfield, NSW 1982; Douglas Fuchs Basketry Workshop, Sydney 1982; Workshop apprentice with Liz Jeneid, Sydney 1982-84; Certificate, School of Colour and Design, Sydney 1983-84; workshops in numerous techniques including Aboriginal basketry 1975-2000.

Related experience: Secretary then President Crafts Council of NSW 1982-85; Board Member Crafts Council of SA 1987-88; President Fibre Basket Weavers of SA Inc 1990.

Exhibitions and awards: recent solo: JamFactory Craft and Design Centre, Adelaide 1999; Old Bakery Gallery, Lane Cove, Sydney 1999; Brisbane City Art Gallery, Qld 1999; Smyrnios Gallery Australia, Melbourne 2000; recent two-person exhibitions: Baskets, Bowls and Botany, Bungendore Wood Work Gallery with Robert Howard; numerous group exhibitions including recent: Meroogal Women's Art Prize, Historic Houses Trust of NSW, Nowra, 1999 (winner); Tactile Art Prize, Royal Blind Society, Customs House, Sydney 1999; Contemporary Basketry in Australia, Lismore Regional Gallery, NSW 1999; Alice Springs Craft Acquisitive, Alice Springs, NT 1999; Skill, Craft Vic. Travelling Exhibition 1999; Small-Scale, Maudspace, Sydney 1999; Too Weave, Broken Hill City Art Gallery, NSW 2000.

Collections and commissions: Historic Houses Trust of NSW, Australian Museum; American Collectors Circle; Alice Springs Craft Acquisition, NT; Art Gallery of SA; Vic. State Craft Collection; Ararat Gallery Permanent Textile Collection, Vic., Powerhouse Museum, Sydney and others; private collections in UK, Japan, USA, India, New Guinea, Singapore, Australia, Canada, NZ, Germany, Italy, Holland; Human Rights and Equal Opportunity Commission 10th Anniversary Award piece 1994; 1840s willow crib, Historic Houses Trust of NSW, Sydney 1993.

Elizabeth Kelly 127
Woodville South, SA

Studied: Glass Workshop Trainee JamFactory Workshops Inc, South Australia 1987; Bachelor of Visual Art in Glass, Institute of the Arts, Australian National University 1991; Master of Visual Art, Sydney College of the Arts, University of Sydney 1997.

Teaching and related experience: demonstrator, Glass Studio, Sydney College of the Arts, University of Sydney 1992; research assistant in coloured glass, Sydney College of the Arts 1993; lecturer, part time lecturer and tutor, Glass studio, Sydney College of the Arts 1993-97; Head, Glass Studio, JamFactory Contemporary Craft and Design, Adelaide 1997-.

Exhibitions and awards: recent solo: Sydney College of the Arts Gallery 1997; Side On Gallery, Sydney 1997; JamFactory Gallery 1998; Beaver Gallery, ACT 1999; numerous group exhibitions, including 1999: JamFactory; Nexus Gallery, SA; University College, Launceston, Tas.; Galleria Marina Barovier, Venice, Italy; Ausglass selected Members Exhibition, Wagga Wagga City Art Gallery; Craft Qld, Brisbane. Collections: Art Bank, NSW; Australian National University Glass Collection, Canberra.

Sally King 97
Ulverstone, Tas.

Born Tas. 1938

Studied: trained as a nurse and worked as sister at Red Cross Hospital, Melbourne; involved in Red Cross handcrafts and practised many crafts including cane basketry; attended Douglas Fuchs' 'Floating Forest' exhibition and workshop in Melbourne in 1982.

Teaching experience: taught basketry for a number of years.
Related experience: fulltime basketmaker since 1989, selling through craft markets and other retail outlets.

Deborah Kneen 29
Jewfish Bay, NSW

Born Sydney 1952

Studied: University of Sydney, B.A. Dip Ed 1971-74.

Teaching experience: Modern languages, Sydney high schools 1975-85. Painting classes in Australia from 1987 and recently NZ, UK and France. Accredited teacher FDAA, Inc. Presented segments on folk art for Foxtel's Lifestyle Channel 1998.

Awards: Finalist (Honorable Mention) DAC Awards (US Society of Decorative Painters) 1995

Publications: author or co-author of numerous books on craft and decorative painting, including: Folk Art of France, Handpainted Heirlooms, The Art of Teaching Craft (with Joyce Spencer) and The Painted Bouquet Volumes I-III (with Christine Whipper). Editor of a series of folk art magazines. Columnist since 1996 for Folk Art and Decorative Painting magazine. Contributor to many Australian craft magazines and The Decorative Painter (US).

Full member Australian Society of Authors and Honorary Life Member Friends through Folk Art Guild, Inc.

John Lloyd 131
Lloyd Murray Glass
Byron Bay, NSW

Born Adelaide, SA

Studied: Qualified Moulder's Certificate in Sand Moulding and lost cast wax process; apprentice at Bradford Steel Foundries, Adelaide 1974-78.

Related experience: Ballina Slipway Foundry, experience in moulding using a variety of metals including bronze, aluminium, cast iron, steel and involved in making pieces for vintage cars, ships, bells rudders, cast iron lacework, intricate figurines and statues 1980-83; making furniture from Tas. Oak at Zentai Futons 1983-86; Full time glass blowing and creating exhibition pieces for various Australian and overseas galleries, Colin Heaney Hot Glass 1987-93; Working with Geoff Murray to establish and develop Lloyd Murray Glass 1995 - .

Exhibitions and awards: represented nationally from Darling Harbour to Port Douglas to Norfolk Island and in private collections in Australia and overseas.

Will Matthysen 71
Warrandyte, Vic.

Born South Africa 1954

Arrived Australia 1989

Studied: University of Witwatersrand, Johannesburg, B.Arch. 1974-77; Architectural Association, London, Diploma 1979-82; RMIT University, Melbourne, Master of Design 1990-92; RMIT, Melbourne, Clock and watchmaking, 1993.

Related experience: architect London, Hong Kong, Melbourne 1982-89; established wood workshop, Melbourne 1989.

Teaching experience: Architecture and Design part time RMIT University, Melbourne 1989-93; Architecture and Design part time Melbourne University 1993-94.

Awards and exhibitions: (Prizewinner) Sculpture/Carving and working with wood, Exhibition Buildings, Melbourne 1991; First prize, Sculpture/Carving, Vic. Woodworkers Association Exhibition, Melbourne 1991; First prize Sculpture/Carving and working with wood, Melbourne 1992; Times change. About time. Makers Mark Gallery, Melbourne 1993;

Don Metcalfe 81

Rock Valley, NSW

Born Brisbane 1953

Self-taught

Exhibitions: Chocolate Factory Arts Centre 1994-96; Maudespace, Blackwattle Studios, Glebe, Sydney 1994; Trinity Art and Craft Festival, 1995; Beefweek Arts Exhibition 1995 (Prizewinner).

Gallery exhibitions and sales: Bungendore Woodworks Gallery, Bungendore, NSW; Naturally Australian, The Rocks, Sydney; Leura Fine Woodwork Gallery, Leura, NSW; Griffith Furniture Gallery, Murwillumbah, NSW; Gallery D, Montville Qld; Robin's Nest, Mount Tambourine, Qld.

Jeff Mincham 99

Cherryville, SA

Born Milang, SA 1950.

Studied: SA School of Art 1970-73; postgraduate studies Tas School of Art 1974.

Teaching experience: guest lecturer and demonstrator in Australia and overseas, including more than 100 workshops and summer schools conducted in all states and in the UK, USA and NZ; guest demonstrator, Raku Ho'olaul'ea, Hawaii 1994; guest lecturer, Glasgow School of Art 1996; judge of more than 20 major art and ceramic awards throughout Australia and in NZ.

Exhibitions and awards: 56 solo exhibitions since 1976 in Australia and USA; participated in more than 120 group shows, survey and touring exhibitions in Australia, USA, NZ, Italy, France, Japan, China, the Netherlands and Germany; winner of numerous awards and prizes in Australia and overseas including honourable mention, 3rd Mino International Ceramics Award, Nagoya, Japan 1994; winner Nillumbik Art Award 1995; Stanthorpe Arts Festival Sculpture Award 1996; award winner Newcastle Regional Gallery Award 1997; winner SA Ceramics Award.

Publications: regular contributor to Pottery in Australia; major articles in Craft Arts International 1985 and 1992, Ceramic Art and Perception 1991; articles in many books and other journals.

Nick Mount 125

Leabrook, SA

Born Adelaide, SA 1952

Studied: SA School of Art 1970-71; Gippsland Institute of Advanced Education, non diploma course in Visual Arts 1972-74; studied glass in Europe and US 1975.

Teaching experience: has demonstrated and taught glass techniques since 1974 including as tutor at Caulfield Institute of Technology, Melbourne 1976; Ausglass Conference 1981; Pilchuck School, Washington State, USA 1987, 93, 95 and 99; part time University of SA 1992; workshops Sydney College of the Arts 1996, Sheridan College, Toronto, Canada 1997; Glass House, Wertheim, Germany 1998; Nijima Glass Centre, Japan 1998.

Related experience: residencies: University of SA 1997; Californian College of Arts and crafts 1997; Canberra Institute for the Arts 2000; established and operated own glass studios - One Off, Vic. 1977; Budgeree Glass 1978-91; Norwood Studio 1991; Head of Hot Glass Studio, JamFactory Contemporary Craft and Design Centre, Adelaide 1994-97.

Exhibitions and awards: more than 120 solo and group exhibitions

---

Best overall piece, Warburton Winterfest 1993; First prize, Vic. Woodworkers Association 1997; First prize, Vic. Woodworkers Association 2000.

Geoffrey Murray 131

Lloyd Murray Glass

Byron Bay, NSW

Born Newcastle, NSW

Studied: Newcastle Technical College, School of Art and Design part time 1975-76, full-time majoring in painting 1978-79; University of Tas. School of Art, Bachelor of Fine Arts majoring in Ceramics with unit of Hot Glass 1980-84.

Related experience: Decorative and functional leatherwork with Appaloosa Leather in Newcastle 1973-78; Wood-Fired Stoneware in Byron Bay 1984-90; Full time glass blowing at Colin Heaney Hot Glass 1990-95; Working with John Lloyd to establish and develop Lloyd Murray Glass 1995 -.

Exhibitions and awards: represented nationally from Darling Harbour to Port Douglas to Norfolk Island and in private collections in Australia and overseas; winner of Byron Shire Art Class Acquisitive Prize for stoneware in 1980s.

Silvana Natoli 13

Sydney, NSW

Born Sydney 1956

Studied: fashion at East Sydney Technical College; découpage with Val Lade from 1994.

Related experience: working in family business.

Teaching experience: Chatswood Community Evening College 1996-98; Lindfield Decorative Arts Centre 1998; first Artist in Residence Découpage Guild of NSW 1996-2000, taking many classes and workshops for the Guild.

Exhibitions and awards: exhibited with the Découpage Guild of NSW since 1995; many awards from Découpage Guild of NSW.

Publications: numerous projects published in magazines.

Richard Raffan 67

Tharwa, ACT

Born UK 1943

Arrived in Australia 1983

Studied: Fine Arts, Exeter College of Art, UK 1962-3.

Related experience: design and manufacturing experience, Desmond Sawyer Designs 1961; worked London wine trade, managing wine and retail stores 1965-69; began turning wood 1970, acted as consultant on all aspects of woodturning to quangos, small businesses and individuals; serves regularly on selection and adjudication panels for exhibitions.

Teaching experience: Craftsman in Residence, Sturt Workshops, Mittagong, NSW 1977; Artist in Residence, University of Tas. 1984; since 1978 in constant demand as a workshop leader, demonstrator and key presenter in Australia, USA and UK, appearing regularly in schools, colleges, universities, woodworking and woodturning associations but also including: Royal College of Art, London; Brigham Young University, USA; Connemara West, Ireland; Canberra School of Art; Highland Craftpoint, Scotland; Parnham Foundation, UK; RMIT, Melbourne.

---

throughout Australia, NZ, Japan, South America, USA, Germany, Netherlands, Italy, Portugal 1977-2000 including SOFA 1994, 95, 96; first prize Glass Section, Stirling and District Council Art and Craft Award 1983; recipient of Gold Medal, Bavarian State Award, Munchen, Germany 1997.

Collections and commissions: National Gallery of Australia, state and regional galleries in Australia, Art Bank, Powerhouse Museum, Parliament House, State Craft Collection, Vic., Glasmuseum, Ebeltoft, Denmark.

Artists' Biographies

Exhibitions and awards: more than 120 major one man shows and group exhibitions since 1970 in Australia, USA and UK including most recently: University of Technology, Sydney 1999; Distelfink Gallery Melbourne (solo) 1999; Bungendore Woodwrks 2000; Canberra Crafts Council 2000; Brigham Young University, Utah, USA 2000; awarded British Crafts Council Loan award 1975; South West Arts Major Award, UK 1980. Collections: represented in numerous public and private collections including British Crafts Council, London; New Parliament House Collection, Canberra; National Gallery, Canberra; Powerhouse Museum, Sydney; Victorian State Crat Collection.
Publications: subject and author of numerous magazine and journal articles; author books (all published in USA) Turning Wood with Richard Raffan 1985; Turned Bowl Design 1986; Turning Projects 1991; Turning Boxes with Richard Raffan 1998; Turning Wood with Richard Raffan, 2nd edition, 2001; several woodturning videos.

Kirstie Rea 133
Canberra, Australia
Studied: various stained glass courses 1976-80; Bachelor of Arts (Visual), Canberra School of Art, Australian National University 1986; various workshops in kilnwork, printmaking from glass etc 1988-93.
Teaching experience: various including part time lecturer, Canberra Institute of the Arts Glass Workshop 1987-99; Studio ARC Teaching tour of USA - Portland Oregon, Corning Studio New York, Urban Glass New York 1999; teaching workshops USA and Europe 2000.
Related experience: established studio 1987; artist in residencies: Bullseye Glass Co, USA 1994; Wanganui Polytech NZ 1999; Bullseye Glass 2000.
Exhibitions and awards: numerous including recent solo: Quay School of the Art Gallery, Waganui NZ 1999; recent group: Canberra Glass, Beaver Galleries 1999; Quadrivium Gallery 1999, 2000; Brisbane City Gallery 1999, 2000; Object Galleries Sydney 1999, 2000; Galerie Handwerk, Munich 2000; Axia Modern Art, Melbourne 2000; Canberra Times Critics Circle Award 1996, 1999; Vicky Torr Ausglass Award 1999.
Collections: Art Gallery of WA; Vic. State Craft Collection, Latrobe Valley Art Centre; private collections in USA, Japan and Australia.

Helen Richardson 95
Macclesfield, SA
Born Maidenhead, England 1930
Studied: Art and Craft Certificate, Marleston School of Wool and Textiles 1980.
Teaching experience: various, from Guilds to WEA.
Exhibitions: numerous group exhibitions between 1983 and 1999, including those at the Crafts Council of SA; Distelfink Gallery, Vic. 1984; Royal SA Society of Arts 1989; Adelaide Botanic Gardens 1989, 1994; Prospect Gallery, SA 1994, 95, 98, 99.
Publications: author/editor book Fibre Basketry Homegrown and Handmade 1989.

Jill Roberts 77
The Deepings Dolls
Tas.
Studied: University of Tas., Bachelor of Fine Arts (majoring in painting), Diploma of Education (Visual Arts) 1990.
Related experience: Has worked with deaf children, youth theatre, and in schools, also briefly as a clown; first love is three-dimensional work including the research necessary for accurate costuming of The Deepings Dolls; other art practice includes sculptural paper casting of masks, dragons, coffee tables, the human form.
Teaching experience: art and theatre skills; training of new painters for

The Deepings Dolls.
(See also Adrian Hunt)

Nerida Singleton 17
Brisbane, Qld
Born Kingaroy, Qld 1948
Studied: Arts, University of Qld 1971-74. Worked in husband's veterinary practice until being persuaded to try découpage in 1979.
Teaching experience: conducted seminars and workshops in all Australian states, California and NZ.
Exhibitions and awards: Noosa Regional Gallery; State Library of Qld; Australian Craft Show for 10 years, in all capital cities; one of the Feature Artists with the Australian Needlework, Art and Craft Fair 2000.
Publications: author numerous books on découpage since 1990; various articles and projects for magazines.

Hiroe Swen 111
Queanbeyan, NSW
Born Kyoto, Japan 1934
Arrived Australia 1968
Studied: Kyoto Crafts Institute and five year apprenticeship to Master Potter H. Hayashi, Kyoto.
Teaching experience: various workshops, private classes and residencies throughout Australia 1968 - ; lecturer in residence Seika Art University, Kyoto, Japan 1998; Australian National University Institute of the Arts 1980-99; Visiting Fellow to Australian National University Institute of the Arts 1999 - .
Exhibitions: nine major solo shows at own Pastoral Gallery 1973 - ; numerous solo including recent: Gallery ANRI, Nagoya, Japan 1993; Japanese Garden Centre, Cowra 1995; recent group including: Galerie b15 Handwerk, Munich, Germany 1997; Kuntgewerbe Museum, Dresden, Germany 1997; Museum of ceramics, Sevres, France 1997; Friends at the Edge, Gallery East, Fremantle WA 1999.
Collections: National Gallery of Australia; state and regional galleries; Government House, Canberra; Australia Council, Sydney; High Court, Canberra; Australian Embassies in Washington, Tokyo, New Delhi; Department of Foreign Affairs, Canberra; New Parliament House Collection, Canberra; Australian National University, Canberra; Powerhouse Museum, Sydney; Canberra University; Japanese Embassy, Canberra; Art Bank and private collections in Australia, NZ, Japan, USA, France, England, Germany and Mexico.

Marlene Thiele 91
Adelaide, SA
Born Adelaide, SA 1936
Studied: enrichment courses in copper work, quiltmaking, contemporary embroidery, stained glass, leatherwork and pottery 1973-75; Department of Further Education Art and Craft Certificate, drawing and design with enamelling and printmaking, silver jewellery and sculpture 1975-79; WEA natural basketry course 1985; various workshops with visiting American artists 1995-99.
Teaching experience: various tutoring posts and workshops held in Dookie, Vic., Modbury, SA, Swan Hill, Vic., Balaklava Courthouse Gallery, Waikerie, South Australia; workshops for Fibre Basket Weavers of SA 1995; Melrose Fibre School 1996.
Exhibitions and awards: numerous including recent group exhibitions: She 3, the Box Factory, Adelaide 1997; Home is where the art is Ill, Artspace, Festival Theatre 1998; Lismore Regional Gallery, NSW 2000; Scotch College Fine Art, Torrens Park, SA 2000; solo exhibitions including: Fragmented, Pepper Street Gallery 1997; featured artist JamFactory shop

1997; Chaffey Theatre Foyer, Renmark, SA 1997; Dame Mary Durack Outback Award 1990; two awards National Craft Acquisition NT 1990.
Collections and commissions: private collections in Australia, USA, Brussels and the UK.

Sue Trytell 55

Queenscliff, Vic.
Born Melbourne, Vic. 1943
Studied: National Gallery Art School, Melbourne 1950s; Royal Melbourne Institute of Technology 1959-60; Caulfield Institute of Technology, Melbourne 1961; Vic. Tapestry Workshop Summer School 1976; many overseas workshops and tutorials.
Teaching experience: private workshops in Vic. and interstate 1976 - ; conducted workshops for National Gallery of Vic.; Australian Society for Education through the Arts ; Caulfield Arts Centre School Holiday Program; Fibre Interchange 1984; Education Department of Vic.; Community Arts Board, Collingwood Education Centre.
Related experience: produces a range of miniature wearable art sold through trade fairs and agencies; various artist-in-residencies including Arts Access, Park Towers Project, South Melbourne and Royal Children's Hospital pilot project as well as other schools and colleges.
Exhibitions: numerous solo, most recently: Glory of Gold, Melbourne; numerous group including most recently: Ballarat Fine art Gallery 1998; Jewish Museum of Australia, Melbourne 1998; Makers Mark, Melbourne 1994; Distelfink Gallery, Melbourne 1993; Australian National Gallery 1993.
Publications: author book Glory of Gold 1995; magazine and journal articles and projects.

David Upfill-Brown 63

Launceston, Tas.
Born Johannesburg, South Africa 1948
Arrived in Australia 1982
Studied: working of stone and wood with Shona sculptors, Zimbabwe 1972-73; John Makepeace School for Craftsmen in Wood, Dorset, England 1979-81; study tour galleries, exhibitions, craft workshops in France and England 1993; study tour galleries and exhibitions Seattle, San Francisco and New York, USA 1998.
Teaching experience: craftsman in residence, TAFE, Canberra 1982; part time lecturer Canberra Institute of the Arts, Australian National University 1986-99; teacher of furniture making and carving at own workshop, Tharwa, ACT 1996-99; Academic Director Australian School of Fine Furniture Ltd, Launceston, Tas. 2000 - .
Related experience: practised as a sculptor, South Africa 1972-77; practised as a sculptor, furniture restorer and designer/maker England 1977-79; set up workshop at Cuppacumbalong Craft Centre 1982-95, ACT; timber agent for Australian timbers 1984-92; team member Metaform Design Technology Project 1999; exhibition judge various Woodworkers Guild exhibitions 1988-99.
Exhibitions: numerous solo and group 1976-99 including recent: Boxes, CSA Gallery, Canberra 1996; Conviviality chair exhibition, Craft ACT 1997; Oberon Woodcraft Exhibition 1997; Cutaway, exhibition of carving, Craft ACT 1999; Ex Hedras, chairs at Canberra Museum and Gallery 1999.
Commissions numerous private and public commissions in Australia and overseas including: Speaker's Chair, House of Representatives, Canberra; Presentation Gavels, Department of PM and Cabinet; Cabinet and Ceremonial Chairs, Defence Force Academy; Dining Room Suite, NZ Embassy; Dining system for Japanese Embassy, Canberra.

Marylyn Verstraeten 135

Melbourne, Vic.
Born Perth, WA 1935
Studied: St Anne's College, Perth 1940-51 with Art as major study; jewellery making, Council of Adult Education, Melbourne 1970; sculpture and bronze casting, Prahran Institute of Technology 1972.
Related experience: Silversmithing, Steeth Silverware Manufacturers 1974.
Exhibitions and awards: numerous solo and group exhibitions including: Tooronga Gallery 1972; Craft Centre, Toorak 1974, 75; Beaver Galleries, ACT 1978, 1981; Sale Regional Gallery 1982; Wildlife Artists Society 1982; Caulfield City Art Gallery 1984; Ballarat Fine Art Gallery 1987; Makers Mark Melbourne 1989; Eltham Wiregrass Gallery 1990, 1994; Association of Sculptors of Victoria 1991, 92; and many others.
Collections and commissions: many commissions for presentations to visiting dignitaries or for industry including: Pacific Dunlop; ICI; Miles Laboratories; Victoria State Government; Tattersall's Tall Ships Bi-Centenary Trophy in silver presented to captains of all vessels; ACTU's golden Presentation Medal.

Julie Whitehouse 35

Brisbane, Qld
Born Brisbane 1953
Studied: Qld University of Technology Diploma in Art Teaching 1970-73; Qld College of Art Diploma of Fine Art 1974-75.
Teaching experience: Qld Education Department 1973-77; Loreto College Head of Art 1978-82; Adult and Children's Painting Workshops 1984-96; Tutor Qld Decorative and Folk Artists Symposia; Villanova College Head of Art 1997; TAFE Adult Education painting courses 1990-98; Tutor in Mediaeval Iconography - University of Southern Qld Mcgregor Winter and Summer Schools 1998-2000.
Related experience: corporate, Church and private commissions including Papal vestments, John Paul II Australian visit; book illustrations and design of greeting cards, découpage papers; millennium design for Catholic Church Brisbane; set design and painting 'A Christmas Carol' musical 1998.
Exhibitions and awards: group exhibitions at Brisbane Institute of Art; Decorative and Folk Artists of Qld; Qld College of Art; Gold Coast Art Gallery.

Photo credits

All photography by Andrew Sikorski unless detailed below.

D. Armstrong p90, p117

Terence Bogue p70, p71, p72, p73.

Merv Cannon p34, p35, p36

Robert Colvin p72

David Cummings p85

Photograph of Jeff Mincham p99 © Federal Capital Press

Victor France p102

Victor France/Viscopy p102, p103, p105,

Robert Frith p108, p109

G. Hancock p11, p98, p99, p100, p101, p124, p125, p126

Noel Hart p128, p129

Marjan Kiewiet p72 photographs 1, 2, p73 photographs 3-7

Kluvanek p116

Greg Piper p84 - 85, p86 - 7

Sergio Santos p40, p58

David Shipard p94

Gene Verstraeten p134, p136, p137

Glen Weiss p20, p23

Peter Zurela p103

MasterWorks